hide this italian book

D1569234

Apa Publications GmbH and Co. Verlag KG
New York Munich Singapore

Contacting the Editors
Every effort has been made to provide accurate information in this publication, but changes are inevitable. The publisher cannot be responsible for any resulting loss, inconvenience or injury. We would appreciate it if readers would call our attention to any errors or outdated information; please contact us: Apa Publications, 193 Morris Avenue, Springfield, NJ 07081, USA. E-mail: hidethisxtreme@langenscheidt.com

First Printing: December 2009
Printed in Singapore

Publishing Director: Sheryl Olinsky Borg
Senior Editor/Project Manager: Lorraine Sova
Writer: Oliviero Martini
Reviewer: Andrew Tanzi
Interior Design: Wee Design Group
Composition: Datagrafix, Inc.
Cover Design: Claudia Petrilli
Illustrator: Tatiana Davidova
Production Manager: Elizabeth Gaynor
Interior Photos: page 10 © 2009 Jupiterimages Corporation, page 87 © Brett Charlton, Used under license from istockphoto.com; © Vladimir Rankovic, Used under license from istockphoto.com; © Jennifer Trenchard, Used under license from istockphoto.com; © Hans F. Meier, Used under license from istockphoto.com; © Arialdo Rescigno, Used under license from istockphoto.com

INSIDE

INTRO

Which would you say or text to your BFF?

a. Hello, would you like to attend a party tonight?
b. Hey dude/bitch, wanna hang out 2nite?

If you picked option a, close this book now (we're warning you!). But, if you picked b, keep on reading…

This book is *not* for people who want to sound like they just got off the plane when they visit Italy. It should be used only by cool people who want to learn how to speak *real* Italian. There are no verb conjugations, no grammar lessons and no rules with all kinds of exceptions. The language included in this book is what young, hip Italians really speak today—and we've made it as easy as possible for you pick up and use. You'll navigate your way through everything from dating and sex to fashion and style.

WHAT YOU NEED TO KNOW

We're assuming that you may already know a little Italian, but it's OK if you don't. The expressions included in this book are translated with their closest equivalent in English—there isn't always a direct translation. We explain everything you need to know, and you can even hear some of the expressions in this book at our website, www.langenscheidt.com/hidethis. Look for: 🔊 . So, you don't only know *what* to say, but *how* to say it!

You may just want to listen to them with headphones so you don't offend anyone…

SEX

Got your attention? Words or expressions followed by ♂ are for guys only and those with ♀ are for girls only.

BOMBS AWAY!

We've labeled the really bad stuff clearly to try and save you from some uncomfortable situations. Here's how it works:

💣 means that you can use these words around your friends and sound cool;
💣💣 are used for words that are completely inappropriate, incredibly offensive and downright dirty! You should only use these words with your closest friends and definitely *not* around Italian old folks, teachers, etc.

FEATURES

You'll also notice these different features throughout the book:

Manga	Cool comics that feature cool Italian language
Dialogue	Conversations between Italian hipsters
Word Bytes	A list of key words from the manga or dialogue
All That Slang	Short sentences, phrases or words for lots of crazy situations
A-List	The best of the best—the shortlist of the hottest things
Use It or Lose It!	Fun activities that get you using the slanguage you've picked up
Quiz	Interactive quizzes that test your personality and knowledge of Italian slang
Mixed Up	An Italian-English game that lets you LOL while practicing your Italian
Q&A	Our very own cultural and language advice column
	For when you want to be naughty or nice
Know-it-all/il Saputello	Interesting facts on Italian slang and culture from our resident nerd.
Gestures	How to say it—visually

DISCLAIMER

There are plenty of phrases in this book that can get you slapped, beat up or smacked down, but there are also plenty of things that can help you make new friends or fall in love with that special someone. It's all about how you decide to use the book. Just don't say we didn't warn you!

AND LAST BUT NOT LEAST...

Languages are constantly evolving—what's in today might be out tomorrow—and while we've done our best to give you the coolest and most up-to-date slang, it's possible that some of the expressions might go out of fashion. So, if you come across anything in this book that's outdated or if you learn a cool new expression that you think we should include in the future, we'd love to hear from you!
Send us an e-mail at: hidethisxtreme@langenscheidt.com.

Cool!

chapter 1

Get info on:

- different ways to say cool
- how to say something sucks

That's cool!

Know-it-all/il Saputello

"Cool" or "cold"—as in temperature—in Italian is **fresco**. Don't use this literal translation to mean "cool" as above.

All That Slang

Although you can say *fico*, here are some other cool words you can also use.

è stupendo	**è troppo bello**
è meraviglioso	**bella lì**
è fantastico	**mitico**

How to say cool in…

Abruzzo
è fregno — it's cool

Calabria
è'na bumm — it's cool

Emilia-Romagna
che sborata 💣💣 — fucking cool

Lazio
che tajo, da paura — how cool, awesome

Lombardia
è figo — it's cool

Sicilia
comanda, spacchiuso — it rules, tasty

Toscana
è ganzo, che spettacolo — it's cool, spectacular

Use It or Lose It!

To express coolness, use these phrases. Just add the cool word of choice.

Che ______________________________!

È una ______________________________!

È ______________________________!

È da paura!
That's really cool!

Che figata!
How cool!

Cazzo che figata! 💣💣
This is fucking great!

Spacca il culo! 💣
That kicks ass!

Cara Chiara:

Last month I went to my cousin's house in Rome. We were talking about a popular British singer and how the singer Giusy Ferreri from Palermo sounds just like him. My cousin kept repeating over and over again "*Che tajo* this song". I don't understand what he meant, since *che tajo* literally means something like "what cut". I don't get it, what is cut?!

Sincerely,
Confuso (Confused)

Caro Confuso:

Don't fuss, *Che tajo* means it's "off the hook" or "very funny". Its original meaning is "to bend over (with laughter)", but it's also used generally to say cool. So, learn the phrase and use it.

Saluti,
Chiara

Cara Chiara:

The other day, an Italian-speaking classmate told me I was very *fica*. When I looked up the word in an online dictionary, I found that *fico* ♂ means fig, and *fica* ♀ means vagina! What does it really mean?

Yours,
Offesa (Offended)

Cara Offesa:

Stai calma. Fico ♂ /*Fica* ♀ also means cool—so you received a compliment! Be aware that, while *fico* ♂ has no sexual connotation, *fica* ♀ can mean a certain female body part, in addition to meaning cool, so use it carefully.

Saluti,
Chiara

Know-it-all/il Saputello

The expression "to keep your cool" can be translated as ***resta calmo.***

Dialogue: Mattia and Katy

MATTIA:	**Ciao Katy!**	Hello, Katy!
KATY:	**Ciao Mattia!**	Hello, Mattia!
MATTIA:	**Che fica che sei oggi…**	You're looking *fica* today…
KATY:	**FICA?** (she slaps him)	*FICA*?
MATTIA:	**Ma… Katy… Fica vuole anche dire cool.**	But…Katy… *Fica* also means cool.
KATY:	**Oops, scusa… non lo sapevo.**	Oops, sorry… I didn't know that.
MATTIA:	(to himself) **Ma pensa te…**	I can't believe it…

What do you think Katy understood?

Use It or Lose It!

How would you say cool if you were…?

1. in any Italian-speaking place
2. in Firenze, Toscana
3. in Milano, Lombardia
4. a potty mouth
5. a nice kid
6. in Emilia-Romagna

1. fico; 2. ganzo, che spettacolo; 3. figo; 4. cazzo che figata, spacca il culo; 5. è da paura; 6. che sborata; remember, you can never go wrong with fico

That's un-cool!

All That Slang

Of course, for every cool thing there is an un-cool thing. Here's how to say that something sucks.

Fa schifo. — It sucks.

Che cazzo di schifo. 💣 — What a load of crap. *You can say* ***cazzo di*** *+ anything (car, work, etc.). To say someone (as opposed to something) is crappy, use* ***sfigato*** *♂/****sfigata*** *♀.*

Schifezza. — Garbage.

Che sfigato ♂/Che sfigata ♀. — He/She's such a loser.

Fa cagare. 💣 — It sucks ass.

Che cazzo di sfigato. 💣💣 — What a fucking loser.

Know-it-all/il Saputello

*The standard way to say something is un-cool is **che brutto** (how ugly). The word for an "un-cool" person is **sfigato** ♂/**sfigata** ♀. **Che palle** is used for boring people and things.*

Use It or Lose It!

What's the right response for each situation? Don't mess up! (No pressure…)

a. Your best friend is showing off a brand-new MP3 player with voice recognition.
b. You're telling your classmates how boring Italian literature classes are.
c. You're showing your sister a horror movie, and she tells you how disgusting it is.
d. Your roommate just sits all day in front of the TV; he doesn't have friends and never speaks.
e. Outside the pub, a stranger is shouting at your friend, and wants to fight him.

1. **Fa schifo!**
2. **Che figata!**
3. **Che palle!**
4. **Che sfigato!**
5. **Stai calmo.**

1. c; 2. a; 3. b; 4. d; 5. e

Word Bytes

You're gonna need to know these for the quiz on the next page!

l'amico	friend	**l'inquilino**	roommate
l'angolo	corner	**l'invito**	invitation
la domenica	Sunday	**la maglietta**	T-shirt
la festa	party	**la maratona**	marathon
il film	movie	**un po'**	a little
grazie	thanks	**qualsiasi cosa**	anything
in casa	at home	**la spiaggia**	beach

Quiz Are you *fico*♂/*fica*♀?

1. If invited to *una festa* you:
  a. check your calendar—you have a lot of *appuntamenti*!
  b. say *scusa*, and then go home to watch a *film* with close *amici*.
  c. go, sit in *un angolo*, then wonder why you went.

2. Your cell phone contact list has:
  a. so many people—including all the *amici* you made while on spring break in Napoli—you don't remember half of them.
  b. good *amici*, *gli inquilini* and the Chinese delivery phone number.
  c. your mom, grandma and aunt on speed dial.

3. Your favorite outfit is:
  a. whatever is in style now—and it always looks *fico* on you.
  b. a classic outfit, like *jeans* and a *maglietta*. You always look clean.
  c. whatever you have on hand: sweat pants, oversized *maglietta*. *Non importa*.

4. Your favorite Italian word for cool is:
  a. *spacca il culo* .
  b. *fico* or *figata*.
  c. *che spettacolo*.

5. *La domenica*, you'd rather:
  a. wake up and continue *la festa*.
  b. go to *la spiaggia*, catch a *filmetto* or enjoy a relaxing day *in casa* on your own.
  c. enjoy *una maratona di film* of your choice with some of your friends.

Mainly As: *fichissimo* ♂/*fichissima* ♀
You are so *fico* ♂/*fica* ♀ you are hot. But careful, some people might think you are too cool to be true!

Mainly Bs: *un tipo* ♂/*una tipa* ♀
You may not party all the time, but you don't care. You do your thing, and that makes you *fico* ♂/*fica* ♀.

Mainly Cs: *un po' sfigato* ♂/*po' sfigata* ♀
Don't try to be *fico* ♂/*fica* ♀—enjoy yourself and others will enjoy spending time with you too. *Tu spacchi* in your own way.

Use It or Lose It!

Off the top of your head—without looking back—name 10 cool and/or un-cool words you now know in Italian. Write down your answers, then try reading your answers aloud in front of a mirror to see how *fico* ♂/*fica* ♀ you look.

Friends & Family

chapter 2

Get info on:

- nicknames and pet names
- meeting people and talking with friends
- slang about family members

All That Slang

Terms for strangers, acquaintances, friends and lovers…

tipo♂/tipa♀

guagliò♂/guagliona♀ (southern Italy)

typical guy/gal

*For a guy or a girl you don't know, use **tizio♂/tizia♀**.*

stronzo 💣💣

asshole

literally, turd

un fico♂/una fica♀ 💣

hottie

*Note: **Fico** and **fica** also mean cool, and are used as adjectives.*

vecchio♂/vecchia♀

friend, buddy *literally, old man*

In southern Italy, say ***fra'***♂ *or* ***cumpa'***♂*; in Veneto,* ***vecio***♂*/****vecia***♀.

fighetto♂/ fighetta♀

snob

This is said about a wealthy or stuck-up kid. You'll hear also ***fichetto/fichetta***.

figlio♂/figlia♀ di papà

richie *literally, daddy's darling*

zitella

spinster

sfigato♂/ sfigata♀

loser

sballone♂/sballona♀

drunk, stoner

This one describes someone who's a lush and/or a pot head—generally an all-around partier.

Use It or Lose It!

Can you find these people in this party scene?

- **tipo**
- **fighetta**
- **zitella**
- **sballone**

Word Bytes

You gotta know these to take the quiz…

l'alcol	liquor	**molto♂/molta♀**	a lot, much
il ballo	dance	**la musica**	music
la famiglia	family	**la nonnina**	grandma
la festa	party	**la personalità**	personality

Quiz What is your *personalità*?

Are you a *fighetto*♂/*fighetta*♀, *tipo*♂/*tipa*♀ or *sballone*♂/*sballona*♀?
Find out.

1. You're enjoying your day at *Rimini* beach on the east coast of Italy by:
- **a.** covering up with SPF 70 and an oversized T-shirt.
- **b.** playing beach volleyball with the *tipi e tipe* next to you. After the game, you and your new friends have a few drinks to celebrate your win.
- **c.** finding the perfect spot far from the crowd, then asking a *fico*♂/*fica*♀ to rub oil on your back.

2. At *la cena di famiglia:*
- **a.** your *nonnina* slips you some money for being so nice—you baked dessert and offered to drive a drunk aunt home.
- **b.** you bring some *vino,* jump around with the kids and leave early to meet your friends.
- **c.** you don't show up; you're tired of the family yapping about how you should get off your ass.

3. *La festa* is:
- **a.** a dinner party with your close friends, which you and your *tipo*♂/*tipa*♀ lovingly prepared together.
- **b.** getting together with friends, where the conversation is as important as the food and drinks!
- **c.** any place with *musica, ballo* and *molto alcol*...

4. *La festa* ends at:
- **a.** 10 o'clock, sharp—you need your eight hours (or more) of beauty sleep.
- **b.** 10, 11, 12, 1—it depends on the party...
- **c.** never!

Mainly As: *fighetto*♂/*fighetta*♀ borderline *sfigato*♂/*sfigata*♀
You want to be perfect and often forget to have fun. People in the office rarely talk to you; they're afraid you will backstab them to get points with the boss. Still, you have a few good friends who really care about you. You won't get skin cancer, but you probably have an ulcer the size of the Colosseum.

Mainly Bs: *tipo*♂/*tipa*♀
You are the life of the *festa*; everybody likes you! When you're not there, people notice. Keep it up and have fun—you only live once!

Mainly Cs: *sballone*♂/*sballona*♀
You're too extreme. Still, there is some hope if you reel it in a little. Also, consider getting strangers to rub some SPF 60 on your back instead of tanning oil.

All That Slang

When you're on a first-name basis with Italian speakers, try out some nicknames. Here are some of the most popular.

NAME	NICKNAME
Alessandro	**Ale, Sandro**
Antonio	**Toni, Tonino**
Domenico	**Mimmo**
Elisa	**Eli**
Elisabetta	**Betta**
Enrico	**Chicco**
Francesco	**France, Cesco**
Giuseppe	**Beppe**
Maria	**Mari**
Salvatore	**Totò, Salvo**
Tommaso	**Tommy**

Ciccio♂ / *Ciccia*♀, *Bello*♂ / *Bella*♀, *Capo*♂ and *Mister*♂, are generic nicknames used regardless of the person's actual name. Diminutives are also popular; just add *-ino*♂ or *-ina*♀ to the end of the name (you may need to drop the last vowel, in some cases), for example: Luigi = Luigino;
Sara = Sarina.

Use It or Lose It!

What are these people's real names?

Totò Chicco Sandro Beppe Sarina

Salvatore; Enrico; Alessandro; Giuseppe; Sara

All That Slang

In case you forget someone's name, avoid embarrassment by using a pet name. You can also use these with your close friends and family. Be careful! Use these sweet little words only with people you know; it would be rude to call a stranger "baby".

amore mio	my love	**caro♂/cara♀**	dear
il mio angelo	my angel	**cucciolo♂/cucciola♀**	kitten
bello♂/bella♀	dude/beauty	**fratello♂**	brother, bro
bimbo♂/bimba♀	baby *Don't worry! **Bimbo** isn't an insult in Italian like it is in English!*	**piccola♀**	cutie *literally, little one*
		tesoro mio	my darling

Cara Chiara:

On my last vacation I went to the south of Italy, and a lot of people approached me with comments about the weather, the news, food, etc. I was afraid it was some kind of plot to steal my identity, so I snubbed them. I've discussed this with many friends and they said they would do the same. But recently, someone said I was paranoid and they were just being friendly. Whaddaya say about this?

Cordialmente (Regards),
Jack

Caro Jack:

People in Italy, and especially in the southern regions, are warm and inviting (of course there are exceptions), and talking to strangers in the street is as normal as drinking coffee in the morning. So don't be afraid to chat with anyone. You don't even have to fear being asked for your mother's maiden name—it's common for Italians to use both their mother and father's last names. But don't give up your social security number.

Buona fortuna (Good luck),
Chiara

Cara Chiara:

When I first met a friend from Rome, he gave me two kisses, one on each cheek. I found it weird, although I was a bit happy, because he obviously liked me. It turned out my friend is happily married and has no interest in me. When I met his wife, she also gave me two kisses. I haven't invited them to my house—I'm afraid they want *una cosa a tre*, a threesome. What should I do?

Spaventata (Scared),
Dolly

Cara Dolly:

Don't be a *sfigata.* It's customary for Italians to kiss as a greeting. Your friend and his wife are most likely from the south, where two kisses are planted with a lot of enthusiasm even on strangers. You won't be expected to kiss anyone but, when someone kisses you, take it with grace. Also, don't be surprised if they call you *cara* or *carissima.* Drop your guard and puck'r up (and don't be too quick to call your harassment lawyer).

Baci
Chiara

Use It or Lose It!

Finish this message using pet names.

__________________ (my love), I just wanted to tell you that Jes and I have decided to be together. Jes is __________________ (my angel). Forgive me, __________________ (my darling), remember that you will always be my __________________ (kitten) and my __________________ (baby).

Amore mio; il mio angelo; tesoro mio; cucciolo♂ / cucciola♀; bimbo♂ / bimba♀

Dialogue: Pettegolezzi

Wanna gossip like the *pettegoli* in this conversation?

ALESSIO:	**Te l'hanno detto?**	Did anybody tell you?
MANUELA:	**Cosa?**	What?
ALESSIO:	**Il tipo dell'appartamento di sotto sta con una nuova…**	The guy from the apartment below has a new partner…
MANUELA:	**Ma dài! Ma come?**	Really? How so?
ALESSIO:	**Si, me l'ha detto Anna. E non indovineresti mai chi è…**	Yes, Anna told me. And you'll never guess who it is…
MANUELA:	**Chi?**	Who?
ALESSIO:	**Il fratello della sua ex!**	His ex-girlfriend's brother!
MANUELA:	**Dio, non ci posso credere.**	OMG, I can't believe it.
ALESSIO:	**Che casino!**	What a mess!

Word Bytes

la bugia	lie
che	what
il pettegolezzo	gossip (info)
il pettegolo♂/la pettegola♀	gossip (person)
sicuro♂/sicura♀	sure
spettegolare	to gossip
la storia	story
il vicino♂/la vicina♀	neighbor

Use It or Lose It!

Can you pass the polygraph? Write *vero* if the statement is true or *falso* if it's not.

1. In the beginning, Manuela does not believe what Alessio is telling her.
2. Manuela told Alessio the *pettegolezzo.*
3. The dude downstairs is dating someone new.

1. vero; 2. falso, Anna told the pettegolezzo to Alessio, and he told Manuela; 3. vero

All That Slang

If you want to know more than you should, you must learn to gossip! Memorize these phrases to get what you want.

Che è successo?	What happened?
Che casino!	What a mess!
Hai sentito l'ultima?	Did you hear the latest news?
Mi hanno detto che…	They told me that…
Non lo sapevo.	I didn't know.
Ho sentito che…	I heard that…
Chi te l'ha detto?	Who told you?

Use It or Lose It!

Finish this juicy bit of gossip.

FRANCESCO: Simona, ____________________? (Did you hear?)

SIMONA: ____________________? (What happened?)

FRANCESCO: Sai quella storia di Toni… (You know that thing about Toni…)

SIMONA: ____________________. (I didn't know.)

FRANCESCO: Ha distrutto la macchina al vicino. (She crashed the neighbor's car.)

SIMONA: ____________________! (What a mess!)

hai sentito l'ultima; Che è successo; Non lo sapevo; Che casino

Know-it-all/il Saputello

*To get more info about **pettegolezzi**, tune in to Italian TV channels or websites like **Italia 1** and **Dagospia**, which frequently show gossip shows. Watch and learn how to gossip like a pro—in Italian!*

Gesture

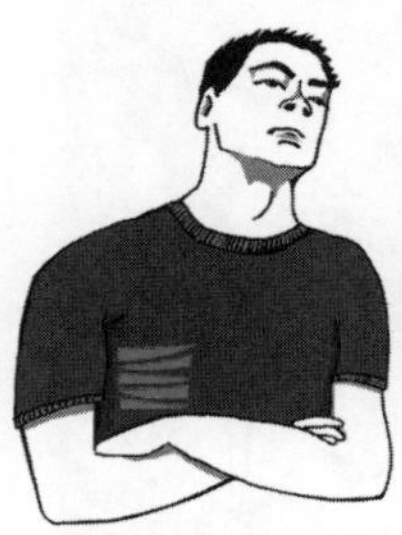

If you want to be confrontational, a slight forward chin movement is all you need to "say" *Che cazzo c'hai?* (What the fuck do you want?)

Andrea's dysfunctional family

Beh?
What?

la nonna che spacca (tatuata)
cool (tattooed) grandma

Ahi!
Ouch!

il nonno pieno di acciacchi
achy grandpa

Mi prendo cura della mia famiglia.
I take care of my family.

la mamma tipica
old-fashioned mom

Dove ho messo gli occhiali?
Where did I put my glasses?

il papà distrattone
forgetful father

Ho preso da mamma.
I take after my mom.

lo zio rocchettaro
rocker uncle

Adoro questa famiglia.
I love this family.

la zia ridicola
ridiculous aunt

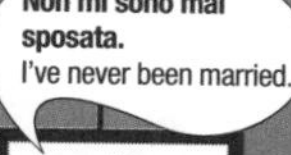

la zia zitella
spinster aunt

La mia famiglia è la migliore del mondo.
My family is the greatest.

Andrea
Andrew

VOGLIO LA MAMMA!
I want my mommy!

il fratellino piagnone
whiny brother

Non sopporto la mia famiglia.
I can't stand my family.

la cugina antipatica
arrogant cousin

Voglio vivere da sola!
I want to live alone!

la cugina darkettona
gothic cousin

Mixed Up

What's wrong with this family scene?

a. name for goth sister
b. name for hot guy ♂
c. name for arrogant brother
d. name for forgetful mom

Carla, the ______________ (a) is waiting for her date to arrive. The doorbell rings. A ______________ (b) is at the door. Carla gets up to greet him, but is intercepted by ______________ (c). Oliviero, the ______________ (c), and the ______________ (b) know each other! Then, the ______________ (d) walks in and says to her daughter, "I thought *you* had a date?!"

All That Slang

Expand your slanguage on family members…

il mio vecchio/la mia vecchia — old man/old lady *These slang terms are used to talk about your parents.*

papi/mami — daddy/mommy

pa'/ma' — pa/ma *Just like in English!*

marito/moglie — husband/wife

nonno/nonna — grandma/grandpa

zietta — auntie

Use It or Lose It!

Can you ID the people in this family picture?

1. ______________________
2. ______________________
3. ______________________
4. ______________________

1. papi; 2. mami; 3. nonna; 4. nonno

Know-it-all/il Saputello

Family is such an important part of the Italian lifestyle, that quite a few family terms have a second, slang meaning. Here are some examples:

Mamma mia!	OMG! *Literally, my mother!*
Soreta! 💣💣	Fuck your sister! *Literally, sister!*
Cuggì!	Buddy! *Literally, cousin! This is a shout out to your friends.*
Fra'!	Bro'! *Literally, brother! This is a another way to call your pals.*
Comare!	Gossip! *Literally, mother-in-law! Ha ha, this one rings true, doesn't it?*

Know-it-all/il Saputello

You've probably heard your Italian relatives and friends use the word ***allora*** *rather frequently.* ***Allora*** *is one of the most useful words for you to learn. It means just about anything—it can be used to gather your thoughts (think: "like" or "um" in English), as an attention grabber (****Allora, andiamo?*** *Come on, let's go!* ***Allora! Basta! Hello-o!*** *Stop it!), as an exclamation (****Gol! E allora! Goal!*** *They're kicking ass!) and so much more. Make sure this gem becomes part of your Italian vocabulary.*

Cara Chiara:

I'm dating *un tipo di Roma*, he's 24, very nice, handsome, polite and has a good job...but he still lives with his *vecchia*! He doesn't come across as a momma's boy, but I just can't get over the fact that she still cooks him breakfast every morning. When's he gonna move out?

Saluti,
Jane

Cara Jane:

This is a very common situation among Italians—we call them *mammoni*, momma's boys. Italians in general—male and female—live at home until they get married. It's a cultural thing. You'll get used to it, too, once his mom starts to spoil you as well!

Chiara

Cara Chiara,

I've been invited to meet my Italian friends at an *occupazione*. What is it?

Curioso
George

Caro George,

The *occupazione* is a popular event in Italy, during which one or more high schools or university buildings are taken over by students as a protest for social or political reasons. These *occupazioni* are generally safe ways to spend the night: Students gather in the faculty buildings to play music, organize parties or hold free events, meetings and other social activities.

Try and go with an Italian friend—*occupazioni* can get a little wild!

Chiara

Know-it-all/il Saputello

Italian speakers often use ***i miei*** *(literally, my own ones) to refer to their parents or to their whole family.*

Gay & Lesbian

chapter 3

Get info on:

- the usual and not so usual terms for "gay"
- gay-friendly phrases

All That Slang

Warning! These terms are insulting when used inappropriately.

♂♂ How to say "gay"…

gay

finocchio 💣
literally, fennel

ricchione 💣

♀♀ How to say "lesbian"…

lesbica

lella

camionista 💣
literally, truck driver

♂♀ How to say "transvestite"…

travestito

travello

travone

Know-it-all/il Saputello

Be PC and use these terms:
gay/omosessuale, lesbica, bisessuale, bisex, transessuale, travestito
No English translations needed, right?! All other terms can be highly offensive, except when used by those in the LGBT community.

Use It or Lose It!

Identify each by their slang name.

1. 

____

2. 

____

3. 

____

4. 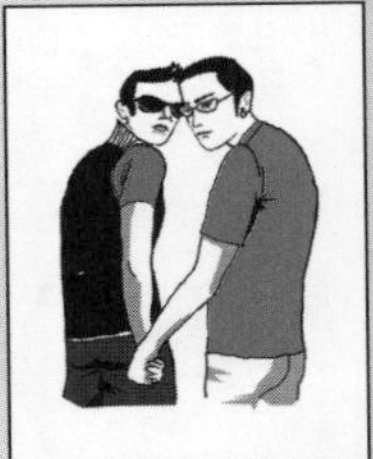

____

1. lelle, camioniste; 2. bisex; 3. travello, travone; 4. finocchi, ricchioni

Know-it-all/il Saputello

The rainbow flag is an international symbol of LGBT acceptance and hard to miss, no matter where in the world you stand.

In some parts of Italy, homosexuals are openly accepted in their community. For example, in Versilia, along the coast of Tuscany, ***gli omosessuali*** *are an integral part of the community. In some other parts of Italy, taboos against homosexuality still exist. Macho stereotypes are still very prominent in some areas, and homosexuality is often not accepted.*

La tresca

Word Bytes

avere una tresca	to have an affair
una tresca	an affair
fare outing	come out of the closet *You might also hear* ***fare coming out.***
È sull'altra sponda.	He/She plays for the other team.

Use It or Lose It!

Do you know what to say in these situations? Select from the phrases below.

1. You just found out… Gianni plays for the other team!
2. You want to know how someone found out Gianni plays for the other team.
3. You want to tell people Gianni is out, finally.
4. You want to say Gianni is having an affair.

a. **Gianni è gay? Come l'hai saputo?**
b. **Gianni ha fatto outing.**
c. **Gianni è sull'altra sponda!**
d. **Gianni ha una tresca.**

1. c; 2. a; 3. b; 4. d

Mixed Up

Put your new vocab to use. Use the LGBT terms to finish the text.

Name a:

a. term for lesbian b. term for bisexual c. term for gay

Mario and Serena broke up because Serena is a ______________ (a). She wanted to date Lucia. But Lucia was really straight, not a ______________ (b) or ______________ (a). After his failure with Serena, Mario thought he might try being a ______________ (c).

Gesture

Flip your ear like this and you'll proclaim someone gay, without actually saying it.

So gay!

All That Slang

If you're gay, some of these phrases may help you get lucky or meet gay friends. If not, read on to be in-the-know on gay culture.

Ho molti amici gay.	I have many gay friends.
È attivo.	He's a top. *Literally, He's active.*
È passivo.	He's a bottom. *Literally, He's passive.*
Mi piace stare sotto.	I like to be on the bottom.
Sono versatile.	I'm versatile.
È lei l'uomo della coppia.	She's the man in the relationship.
Mi piacciono gli orsi.	I like bears. ***Gli orsi*** *are atypical gay men who are often ungroomed and unshaven.*
È una pazza/una principessa.	He is a crazy girl/a princess. *These are said of flamboyant men.*
È ambiguo♂/ambigua♀.	He/She is ambiguous.
Gli♂/Le♀piacciono maschi e femmine.	He/She likes both men and women.
Dov'è il locale gay più vicino?	Where's the nearest gay bar?
Dov'è la serata gay?	Where's the gay venue?
Che fai stasera?	What are you doing tonight?
Dove posso trovare un posto con le drag-queen?	Where can I find a drag show?
È la sua copertura.	She/He is his/her cover. *In Tuscany you may hear:* ***fica-specchio****, literally, mirror-pussy.*
Non nascondere la tua natura.	Don't hide your true nature.
Sono fiero di essere gay.	I'm proud of being gay.

Know-it-all/il Saputello

Did you notice in some of the phrases above, the female form was used to describe a man? Italian is a gender-specific language and, in the case of sexuality, speakers can sometimes change the gender forms to indicate femininity or masculinity.

Quiz

Do you come across as straight, gay or bi?

1. You arrive at a trendy Italian locale, visit the tourist office and:

a. ask the clerk: *Dov'è il locale gay più vicino?*

b. ask a girl what she's doing *stasera*, tonight, while checking out that hot guy walking by.

c. flirt with a clerk of the opposite sex.

2. In the historic part of the city, you notice that the nicest café has a rainbow flag sticker on the door. You:

a. go in; you know you'll make friends with the cute waiters.

b. go to the place next door, which has a mix of guys and girls.

c. avoid the place like the plague.

3. You arrive at the town's hottest shopping mall and:

a. you immediately find the jewelry kiosk and buy a rainbow flag necklace with a matching nipple ring.

b. you're torn between buying a tight, sexy shirt and a classic buttondown. You end up getting both.

c. invest in a safe, classic outfit—much like the one you're wearing.

4. You finally meet that perfect someone for a fling. You've chosen:

a. *una pazza*, if you're a guy (you like your men like your drinks; delicious and girly) or a girly girl (if you're a woman).

b. a boy or a girl, *è uguale*.

c. a member of the opposite sex, of course.

Mostly As: homosexual

Sei fiero di essere gay. Enjoy the gay life, baby!

Mostly Bs: bisexual

To some you are *ambiguo. Per te, è uguale.* You like girls and boys.

Mostly Cs: heterosexual

You're either straight or are deep in the closet.

Use It or Lose It!

Did you pay attention? Do you really know what each phrase means? See if you can pair the phrase with its English equivalent.

1. **Sono fiero di essere gay.**	a. She is the man in the relationship.
2. **Ho molti amici gay.**	b. I have many gay friends.
3. **È lei l'uomo della coppia.**	c. I'm proud of being gay.
4. **Mi piacciono gli orsi.**	d. He is her cover.
5. **È la sua copertura.**	e. I like bears.

1. c; 2. b; 3. a; 4. e; 5. d

Know-it-all/Il Saputello

Gay entertainment isn't very popular in Italy, due to prejudice and religious opposition. Nevertheless, Vladimir Luxuria is an Italian transgendered member of Parliament, who also won a famous reality show. And, it was only in 2008 that, for the first time, an openly gay character was included in a national TV series, ***Un posto al sole****.*

A-List

Here's a list of top-rated *film gay*, gay-themed flicks, from Italy.

Saturno contro	Saturn in Opposition
Le fate ignoranti	The Ignorant Fairies
Come mi vuoi	As You Want Me

Cara Chiara,

I'm gay and going on vacation to Rome with my partner. Is it safe for us to be ourselves in public?

Tua,
Principessa

Cara Principessa:

In most of Italy's metropolitan cities, you can comfortably be gay. Also, don't be afraid to ask a young person where the hotspots are. Popular tourist destinations often offer great alternatives to the hetero scene, and the young locals know the best places to go.

Goditela (Enjoy),
Chiara

Cara Chiara,

My boss is obviously gay, but whenever he has an opportunity, he comments on a girl's *culo*, ass. Meanwhile, I know he is dating one of my male colleagues. Is he gay or not?

Sinceramente,
Ambigua

Cara Ambigua,

È una copertura! Being macho is still very much a part of Italian culture. So, even though your boss may be gay, he may feel the need to prove he's a "real man". Keep in mind that Italians are fairly religious and in many ways conservative. This is slowly changing, but coming out of the closet—especially in the workplace—can be difficult.

Un abbraccio,
Chiara

4

Get info on:

- how to land a date
- love advice
- anatomy 101
- how to break up with someone
- your love horoscope

Dialogue: Alessandra and Riccardo's *appuntamento*

Riccardo invites Alessandra out to dinner for their first *appuntamento*, date...

RICCARDO:	**Ciao Ale, sono Riccardo.**	Hi, Alex, it's Riccardo.
ALESSANDRA:	**Ciao Ric, come va?**	Hey, Ricky, how are you?
RICCARDO:	**Bene, bene. Senti, che fai venerdì?**	Good, good. Listen, what are you doing this Friday?
ALESSANDRA:	**Niente di particolare, dimmi tu.**	Nothing special, you tell me.
RICCARDO:	**Dai! Ti va di andare a cena fuori?**	OK! Do you feel like going out for dinner?
ALESSANDRA:	**Certo, perché no!**	Sure, why not!
RICCARDO:	**Benissimo, passo a prenderti alle sette, che ne dici?**	Great, I'll pick you up at 7—is that good for you?
ALESSANDRA:	**Ok, allora aspetto che mi chiami.**	OK, I'll wait for you to call me then.

Word Bytes

l'appuntamento	date
benissimo	great
dire	to say
fare	to do
fuori	out, outside
mi va di...	I feel like...
prendere	to pick up

All That Slang

Things you say when making a date…

Allora che dici, quando ci vediamo?	So what do you think, when can we see each other?
Non vedo l'ora di vederti.	I can't wait to see you. *You can say this to friends as well, but don't use a seductive tone.*
Allora aspetto che mi chiami?	Will you call me then? *Hey! One can wish…*
Ti chiamo.	I'll call you.
Stasera sono libero♂/libera♀.	I'm free tonight. *Hint, hint…*
A domani.	See you tomorrow.
Ci vediamo presto.	See you soon.
Che fai sabato?	What are you doing Saturday?
Senti, tu esci?	Hey, are you going out? *Get straight to the point.*
Piantala di fare lo scemo e portami fuori.	Stop being a fool and ask me out.
Da me non c'è nessuno…	There's no one at my place…
Va bene.	OK.
Passo alle nove.	I'll come at 9. *People in Italy are often late, so 9 might be more like 9:45. Don't feel insulted! Everybody does it.*
Io sono pronto♂/pronta♀. Ti aspetto.	I'm ready. I'll wait for you.
Non posso, mi dispiace…	I'm sorry, I can't…
Ho troppo da fare.	I'm too busy.
Devo lavarmi i capelli.	I have to wash my hair. *Yeah right.*
E che ne dici di domenica?	And how about Sunday?
C'è il mio ragazzo♂/la mia ragazza♀ qui accanto.	My boyfriend/girlfriend is right here.
Rallenta.	Slow down.
Ma come ti permetti?	How dare you?

Use It or Lose It!

Riccardo and Alessandra arranged another *appuntamento*—but it's up to you to arrange their conversation.

________________ **Va bene.**

________________ **Ho troppo de fare.**

________________ **Che fai mercoledì?**

________________ **Ti aspetto.**

________________ **Bene, passo a prenderti alle sette.**

________________ **Che ne dici di venerdì?**

Che fai mercoledì? What are you doing this Wednesday? Ho troppo da fare. I'm too busy. Che ne dici di venerdì? How about Friday? Va bene. OK. Bene, passo a prenderti alle sette. Good, I'll pick you up at 7. Ti aspetto. I'll wait for you.

Nice and naughty pick-up lines...

Sei davvero stupendo♂/stupenda♀.

You're really stunning.

Sei bellissimo♂/bellissima♀.

You look handsome/gorgeous.

Che fico♂/fica♀ che sei.

You're so hot.

This one can go both ways; the feminine can be naughty if you don't know the person, but it's safe if you're talking to someone you know. Say it with a smile though.

Ciao, ti va qualcosa da bere?

Hey, do you feel like having a drink?

Mi sono perso. Dove abiti?

I think I'm lost. Where do you live?

Belle gambe... quando aprono?

Nice legs...what time do they open?

Ci sono 206 ossa nel tuo corpo. Ne vuoi uno in più?

There are 206 bones in your body. You want one more?

Quiz Pronto per un appuntamento all'italiana?

Are you ready for a hot Italian date?

1. You have a date in two hours. You:
  a. take a bath, spray on some perfume—you are *in tiro*, good to go.
  b. take a quick shower and then grab something out of the closet; you have to be quick since you don't know were your date lives.
  c. watch some TV (hey, you took a bath in the morning, that counts), then walk to the bus stop. Your date will meet you at the restaurant.

2. When talking to your dates, you usually feel:
  a. *tranquillo*♂/*tranquilla*♀.
  b. *nervoso*♂/*nervosa*♀.
  c. *indifferente*—you know there is always going to be another date.

3. The *frase per abbordare*, pick-up line, you often use is:
  a. *Sei davvero stupendo*♂/*stupenda*♀.
  b. *Allora che dici, quando ci vediamo?*
  c. *Belle gambe…quando aprono?*

4. When the date is about to end you:
  a. say *Ti chiamo*, then slip him/her a kiss on the cheek.
  b. ask *Che fai venerdì?*
  c. say *Che fico*♂/*fica*♀ *che sei* in a naughty tone.

Mainly As
Congratulations—*Sei pronto*♂/*pronta*♀.

Mainly Bs
You might be ready, but you need more practice.

Mainly Cs
Reschedule. Your manners and attitude need a lot of work before you attempt to date an Italian!

Cara Chiara,
What can I do to get an *appuntamento* from a sexy Italian?
Ed

Caro Ed,
Play hard to get! *Stai tranquillo, non richiamare mai, e non parlare troppo.* In a nutshell that's all you need to do: calm down, never call back and don't talk too much. And remember, Italians are stylish, so be fashionable: *niente calzini bianchi*, no white socks. Of course if it's a one-night stand you are looking for, go for quick touches and sleazy lines.
Con affetto,
Chiara

Word Bytes

In order to have a successful love life, an anatomy lesson is essential.

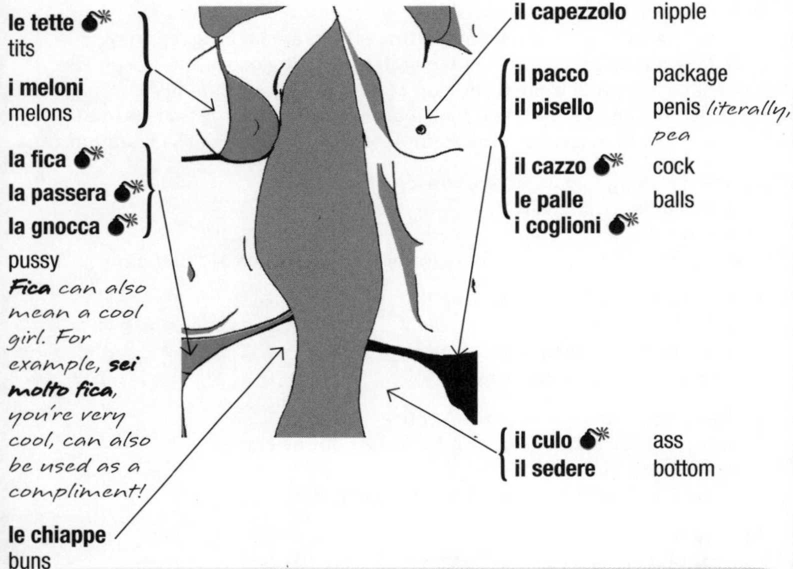
le tette
tits
i meloni
melons
la fica
la passera
la gnocca
pussy
*Fica can also mean a cool girl. For example, **sei molto fica**, you're very cool, can also be used as a compliment!*
le chiappe
buns
il capezzolo nipple
il pacco package
il pisello penis *literally, pea*
il cazzo cock
le palle balls
i coglioni
il culo ass
il sedere bottom

Use It or Lose It!

You've gotta know your body parts. Go ahead and ID 'em.

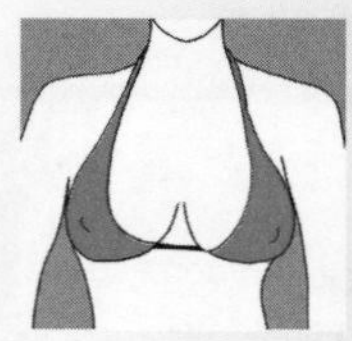

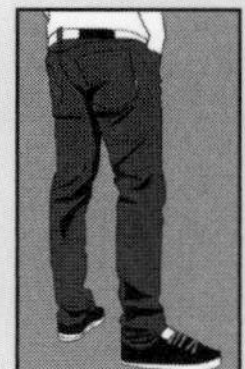

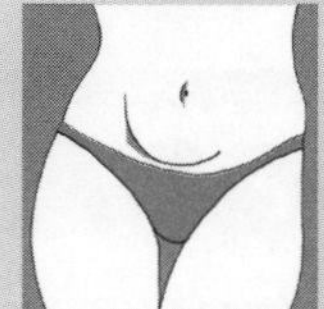

1. ______________________________
2. ______________________________
3. ______________________________
4. ______________________________

1. le tette; 2. il culo; 3. il pacco; 4. la fica

All That Slang

Terms for foreplay…

baciarsi	to kiss
sbaciucchiarsi	to kiss all over
slinguare	to French kiss
strusciarsi	to rub against each other
spogliarsi	to get undressed

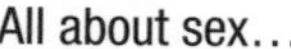

All about sex…

sverginare	to take someone's virginity
fare sesso	to have sex
andare a letto	to go to bed
fare l'amore	to make love
farlo	to do it
avercelo duro	to have a hard-on
scopare	to fuck
ficcare	to fuck *Used in Southern Italy.*

Other sex actions…

succhiare	to suck
sucare	to suck *Used in Southern Italy.*
venire	to come

Going solo…

toccarsi	to touch oneself
farsi una sega	to jack off *literally, go for a hand-saw*
usa Federica, la mano amica	give yourself a hand-job *literally, use Federica, the friendly hand*

Positions…

missionaria	missionary
alla pecorina	doggy style
la forbice	scissors *one alternative, search the Kama Sutra for info…*
da dietro	back door *meaning from behind*

Gestures

Banged somebody lately? Were you the one banged? With this fist move, everyone will understand.

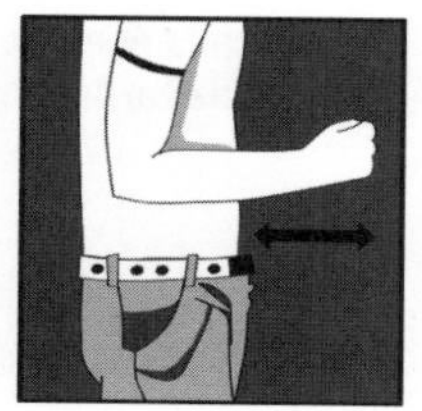

💣 Push your tongue to your cheek then move it around; *sesso orale*, oral sex, is the intention. It's as sleazy as it sounds.

💣 This is called the "L" rule, according to which short men have a long penis, and tall ones have a short one. Very likely, short men created it.

💣 A caress with your finger on somebody's palm is an open invitation *a farlo*.

Use It or Lose It!

Il cubetto di ghiaccio (the ice cube): Try this fun game of foreplay—in Italian—at a party, a bar, a club or whenever you're in the mood. Form a circle of guys and girls. Place a stack of cards with Italian sayings on them (see below for suggestions) in the middle of the circle, along with a large cup of *cubetti di ghiaccio*, ice cubes. Select randomly who begins; he/she has to put *il cubetto di ghiaccio* in his/her mouth, and pass it to whomever he/she wants. *Il cubetto di ghiaccio* must be passed mouth-to-mouth! The ice melts quickly, and the person who can't pass it anymore because it's completely melted has to select a card from the center of the circle and perform the act listed on the card. Here are some suggestions:

bacia la persona alla tua sinistra/destra	kiss the person on your left/right
bacia con la lingua la persona davanti a te	French kiss the person in front of you
togliti qualcosa di dosso	take off an article of clothing
lecca la persona alla tua sinistra/destra	lick the person on your left/right

Una serenata

ANNA! Ti amo.
ANNA! I love you.
Amore!
My love!
Tesoro!
Darling!
Che sdolcinato!
How tacky!
Non ti sopporto più, Antonio.
I can't stand you anymore, Antonio.
Perchè non ti levi dai piedi?
Why don't you get lost?
Annaaaaaaa! Perchè?
Annaaaaaaa! Why?

Word Bytes

amore	love
levarti dai piedi	get lost *said in anger*
sdolcinato ♂ / **sdolcinata** ♀	tacky, cliché, sappy
sopportare	to tolerate
tesoro	darling *literally, treasure*

Know-it-all/il Saputello

*Being **sdolcinato** means being too cliché, that is, overly romantic and sappy. For example a **serenata** (serenade) is **sdolcinata**. Sometimes being **sdolcinato** ♂/**sdolcinata** ♀ works, sometimes it doesn't. It all depends on you and the person you're dating. Some people like sappy love, some don't.*

Use It or Lose It!

Anna needs your help to deliver these lines in the correct order. What should she say first, next and last to get rid of Antonio? She also forgot some words, so you'll have to fill in the blanks.

Perché non ti _______?   Che _____!   Non ti _____, Antonio.

1. Che sdolcinato! How tacky! 2. Non ti sopporto più, Antonio. I can't stand you anymore, Antonio.
3. Perché non ti levi dai piedi? Why don't you get lost?

All That Slang

Talking about *amore* (or getting out of it) is sometimes difficult, especially if you don't know the language. Here are some good-to-know phrases.

Ti amo. I love you.

Ti voglio bene. *There's no exact translation for this one. Think of it as love for family or friends, or use it when you're not quite ready to say I love you. Basically it is love without sexual attraction.*

Mi piaci. I like you.

Ti voglio. I want you.

Ti odio. I hate you.

Vattene! Go away!

Non sei tu, sono io. It's not you, it's me.

Disgraziato♂/Disgraziata♀! You jerk!

Che palle di uomo (to a man)/ **Che palle di donna** (to a woman)! What a loser! *Meaning a person who's boring as hell.*

What kind of a relationship are you in—or do you want?

È il mio trombamico♂/ la mia trombamica♀. We're friends with benefits.

Ci vediamo spesso. We see each other a lot. *Not a serious couple yet...*

Stiamo uscendo insieme. We're going out. *It's getting more serious.*

Stiamo insieme. We're boyfriend and girlfriend.

È il mio♂/la mia♀ amante. He/she is my lover.

Siamo fidanzati. We are engaged.

Use It or Lose It!

Can you guess the status of these relationships? Write 'em down—in Italian.

1. Giorgio and Simona are dating frequently.
2. Tommaso and Silvia are boyfriend and girlfriend.
3. Roberto and Leda *scopano* occasionally.
4. Francesco and Paola are lovers.

Si vedono spesso; 2. Stanno insieme; 3. Ogni tanto vanno a letto; 4. Sono amanti.

Quiz

Are you *uno stallone*♂/*una donna bollente*♀?

1. If your date says he likes you because you have a lot of meat on your bones, you shout ____ before storming out.
  a. *Sfigato!*
  b. *Ti voglio!*
  c. *Ti odio!*
  d. A and C

2. If you want to tell your partner you really love him/her, you say:
  a. *Ti amo.*
  b. *Ti voglio.*
  c. *Ti voglio bene.*
  d. A and B

3. If you want to break up with someone, you exclaim:
  a. *Vattene.*
  b. *Scopami.*
  c. *Ti odio.*
  d. *Ti voglio.*

4. *Sverginare* means:
  a. Take someone's virginity.
  b. Be a sex addict.
  c. Be liberal.
  d. B and C

5. You are *sdolcinato*♂/*sdolcinata*♀ if you:
  a. give your partner an awesome gift on his/her anniversary.
  b. design a postcard using glitter and send it to your date with a singing telegram.
  c. Take your date to a fancy restaurant.
  d. Open the door for your date.

1. d; 2. d; 3. a; 4. a; 5. b

Il tuo oroscopo

Will you be lucky in love? See what the stars say. In case you get lost:

- Keywords are in bold in both languages.
- *Numero fortunato* = lucky number.
- There is a visual guide to colors that complement you.

Ariete ♈

Sicuri di sé, spesso esagerano. Quindi prima presentatevi, e poi toccate **il culo**.

You're very self-confident, and often go too far. So before you touch someone's **ass**, introduce yourself.

Colore: grigio (gray)

Numero fortunato: sette (7)

Toro ♉

A letto siete dei tori, e volete sempre **scopare**, ma in una coppia bisogna adattarsi. Se state con un/una vergine, forse dovrete essere un po' **sdolcinato**♂/**sdolcinata**♀ all'inizio.

In bed you are like a bull and you always want to fuck, but as a couple, you need to be flexible. If you are with a virgin, perhaps you'll have to be **very sweet** at the beginning.

Colore: rosso fuoco (fire red)

Numero fortunato: cinque (5)

Gemelli ♊

Stare con un Gemelli è come stare allo stesso tempo con il vostro **ragazzo**♂/la vostra **ragazza**♀ e il vostro♂/la vostra♀ **amante**. Praticamente un'orgia.

To be with a Gemini is like being with your **partner** and your **lover** at once. Basically an orgy.

Colore: indaco (indigo)

Numero fortunato: due (2)

Cancro ♋

Evitate i **trombamici**. E basta con le **frasi per abbordare**.

Avoid **friends with benefits**. Stop it with those **pick-up lines**.

Colore: verde (green)

Numero fortunato: quattro (4)

Leone ♌

Gli **appuntamenti** non fanno più per voi. Guardatevi attorno: è pieno di **tette** (o **pacchi**, se siete ragazze).

You are done with **dating**. Look around: there are **tits** everywhere (or **packages**, if you're a girl).

Colore: giallo (yellow)

Numero fortunato: dieci (10)

Vergine ♍

Se il vostro **tipo**♂/la vostra **tipa**♀ è un toro, a questo punto dovrebbe già avervi **sverginato**♂/ **sverginata**♀: buon divertimento!

If your **boyfriend/girlfriend** is a Taurus, by now he/she should have **taken your virginity**: have fun!

Colore: viola (purple)

Numero fortunato: nove (9)

Bilancia ♎

È ora di **farlo** in modo diverso…

Time **to do it** in a different way…

Colore: rosa (pink)

Numero fortunato: tre (3)

Scorpione ♏

Siate sinceri: niente **baci** romantici, è ora di **slinguare**.

Be true: no romantic **kisses**—it's time to give some **tongue**.

Colore: arancione (orange)

Numero fortunato: otto (8)

Sagittario ♐

Venerdi incontrerete un **mandrillo** (o una **maialina** se siete uomini): avete voglia di **andarci a letto**?

Friday you are going to meet a **male-slut** (or a **slut** if you are male): do you feel like **going to bed** with him/her?

Colore: nero (black)

Numero fortunato: zero (0)

Capricorno ♑

Il vostro **tipo**♂/ **tipa**♀ ha un **amante**.

Your **boyfriend/girlfriend** has a **lover**.

Colore: blu mare (marine blue)

Numero fortunato: uno (1)

Acquario ♒

L'acqua vi porterà fortuna: incontrerete qualcuno al mare o in piscina, di cui vi **innamorerete**.

Water will be lucky for you: at the swimming pool or at the seaside, you'll meet someone you'll **fall in love with**.

Colore: bianco (white)

Numero fortunato: sei (6)

Pesci ♓

Se non volete più vedere il vostro♂/ la vostra♀ **ex**, siate sinceri♂/ sincere♀ e smettetela di dire che dovete lavarvi i capelli.

If you don't want to see your **ex** anymore, be sincere and stop saying you have to wash your hair.

Colore: grigio (gray)

Numero fortunato: undici (11)

Use It or Lose It!

What is your best astrological match?

1. Who feels like going out for a date?
   a. **Leone**
   b. **Cancro**
2. Who's more fun to go out with?
   a. **Gemelli**
   b. **Pesci**
3. Who's going to be the best match for a night of passion?
   a. **Toro**
   b. **Capricorno**
4. Who should be together?
   a. **Vergine e Toro**
   b. **Leone e Cancro**

1. b; 2. a; 3. a; 4. a

Use It or Lose It!

What are their signs—in Italian?

1. Gabriella is not very creative in bed.
2. Andrea has the energy of a bull.
3. Lina's best color is marine blue.

1. Bilancia; 2. Toro; 3. Capricorno.

chapter

Internet

5

Get info on:

- working with the internet in Italian
- chatting, instant messaging and blogging
- social networking sites, like Facebook® and MySpace®

A high-tech love story

1
Ciao Elena, come va? Ho trovato un sito veramente figo, ti ho mandato il link e la password.
2
Figata! Sono connessa, ora controllo la mail.

3 Oggetto: venerdi sera?
Da: figo_82@htbx.com
A: cybertipa@htbx.com
Ciao, ho visto il tuo profilo su trovamici.htb. Mi piacerebbe conoscerti. Ti andrebbe di uscire a cena venerdi sera? Mandami una mail oppure becchiamoci online. Fai click sul link per chattare.

4
Mi ha risposto all'istante!
Mi metto subito in chat!

5
Elena, ho un appuntamento!
6
Anche io!

7
È stasera alle sette. Al Vicolo.
8
Cosa?! Ma sei tu figo_82@htbx.com?

1 Hey Elena, what's up? I found a super cool website; I forwarded the link and the password. **2** Cool! I'm connected and I'm checking my email. **3** Subject: Friday night? From: figo_82@htbx.com To: cybertipa@htbx.com Hi, I saw your profile on trovamici.htb. I'd love to meet you. What about dinner on Friday night? Send me an email, or let's chat online. Click on the link to chat. **4** He already wrote back! I'm going to chat right now! **5** Elena, I've got a date! **6** Me too! **7** It's tonight at 7. Al Vicolo. **8** What!? You're figo_82@htbx.com?

Word Bytes

cancellare	to delete
chattare	to chat
controllare	to check
da	from
essere connesso ♂ / connessa ♀ a Internet	to be connected to the internet
fare click, cliccare	to click
l'indirizzo	address
inviare, mandare, spedire	to send
la mail/la posta elettronica	e-mail
rispondere	to reply
il sito web	website *There's more than one way to say this; see the Know-it-all/**il Saputello** on the next page.*
stampare	to print

Use It or Lose It!

Match the pics with their labels.

Fare click. **password** **Sono connessa.** **Controllare la mail.**

1. ____________________

2. ____________________

3. ____________________

4. ____________________

1. Sono connessa. ; 2. Controllare la mail. ; 3. Fare click. ; 4. password

Know-it-all/il Saputello

Did you know that there is no one way of saying webpage in Italian? Here are the many variations you may see:

sito | **sito web**
pagina web | **portale**

Another curious thing: Since most tech-related terms are borrowed from English, there are no accepted spellings, regardless of the efforts of scholars; for example, you'll see ***l'email, l'e-mail, la mail*** *and its literal translation* ***la posta elettronica****. There is something that can be agreed upon, though: the terms for e-mail are all feminine.*

All That Slang

More internet-savvy lingo…

Qual è il link? What's the link?

Sei sicuro di voler uscire? Are you sure you want to quit?

Termina la sessione?/Esci? Do you want to log out?/Exit?

Sta sempre a mandare messaggi/ mandare sms. She is texting so much her fingers hurt. *SMS is pronounced* ***esseh-emmeh-esseh****—stress the* ***s*** *and* ***m****.*

Francesco è un hacker. Francesco is a hacker. *Hacker in Italian is pronounced* ***acker****.*

Giulia scarica un sacco di musica pirata. Giulia often downloads music illegally.

Cerca su Google™. Search Google™.

Mi piace navigare su Internet. I like surfing the net.

La mia connessione internet fa schifo. My internet connection sucks.

Devi abilitare i cookie. You need to enable cookies.

Devi scaricarti un programma. You need to download a program.

Non riesco a trovare la wireless. I can't get a wireless signal.

Puoi comprarlo online. You can buy that online.

Sono un blogger. I'm a blogger.

Stasera ci becchiamo in chat. I'll chat with you tonight.

Quiz: Can you survive the internet in Italian?

1. If you want to access your *account di posta*, you need to:
- **a.** *loggarti*
- **b.** write an *sms*
- **c.** *scaricare*

2. If you surf the net frequently (as much as you blink), then someone might call you:
- **a.** *maniaco*
- **b.** *imbranato*
- **c.** *nerd*

3. If the computer suddenly crashes, you wish you'd:
- **a.** *chiuso i documenti*
- **b.** *scaricato i documenti*
- **c.** *salvato i documenti*

4. What does it mean to *cercare* on the net?
- **a.** search
- **b.** cancel
- **c.** close

1. a; 2. a although some might call you c; 3. c; 4. a

Dialogue: Sonia & Mauro

Listen in on Sonia and Mauro, who are having an everyday conversation.

SONIA: **Pronto?** — Hello?

MAURO: **Ciao Sonia, sono Mauro, come va?** — Hello, Sonia, it's Mauro. How are you?

SONIA: **Amore, ti ho appena mandato** — My love, I just sent you an e-mail

MAURO:	**Non una catena, vero?**	Not a chain, right?
SONIA:	**No, no, è un link per Skype™, così possiamo chattare.**	No, no, it's a link to Skype™, so we can chat.
MAURO:	**Ok, però preferisco il cellulare.**	OK, but I prefer to use the cell.
SONIA:	**Sei proprio antico...apri la mail.**	You're always so old-fashioned... open your e-mail.
MAURO:	**Fatto!**	Done!
SONIA:	**Bene, clicca sul link così possiamo chattare.**	Good, click on the link so we can chat.
MAURO:	**Va bene, ti lascio.**	OK, bye.
SONIA:	**Ciao.**	Bye.

Dialogue: Sonia & Mauro chat

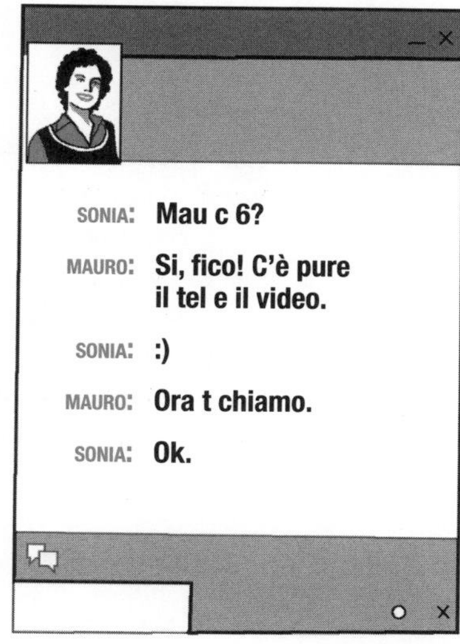

Mau RU there?

Yes cool! There's also phone connection and video.

:)

I'll call u right now.

OK.

All That Slang

If you want to *chattare* or understand *le chat*, follow this guide to basic shorthand.

mi = m; ti = t; ci = c; v = vi	to/for me; you; us; you (plural)
aspetta = asp	wait
comunque = cmq	anyway, however
più = +	more
meno = –	less
perché = xké/xke	why, because
per = x	to, for
non = nn	not
che = ke	that, which
ci sei? = c 6?	RU there? *The number 6 is* ***sei*** *in Italian. It's just like using 2 for to/too in English.*

ti voglio tanto bene = tvtb

I love you loads, I care a lot for you

bacio = smack

kiss

Smack *is what a kiss sounds like, in Italian.*

amore per sempre = amxse

love forever

tutta la notte insieme = tulanoins

together all night long

sei uno zero = 610

you are a loser *literally, you are a zero*

togliti dai piedi = tdp

get out of my way/get lost

Know-it-all/il Saputello

Italians love using shorthand in text messaging; the only problem is there are no rules to follow when using it! The best way to learn some IM shorthand in Italian is to get a lot of text messages from Italian-speaking friends. Don't be afraid to ask for the meaning, because even Italians get confused sometimes! Doing an online search for the meaning of the shortened text could help you out, too; search for ***SMS abbreviazioni****.*

Use It or Lose It!

Learn to text what people want to read... Read the texts aloud and translate them to Italian and then to English.

Giorgio 610 tdp Clau :P	Bene: Io e te tulanoins? amxse smack	tvtb xke c 6
Giorgio: Sei uno zero. Togliti dai piedi. Clau = Giorgio, you are a loser. Get lost. Clau.	Bene: Io e te tutta la notte insieme? Amore per sempre. Bacio. = How about me and you all night long together? Love forever! Kisses.	Ti voglio tanto bene. Perché? Ci sei? = I care a lot for you. Why? Are you there?

Social Networking, in italiano

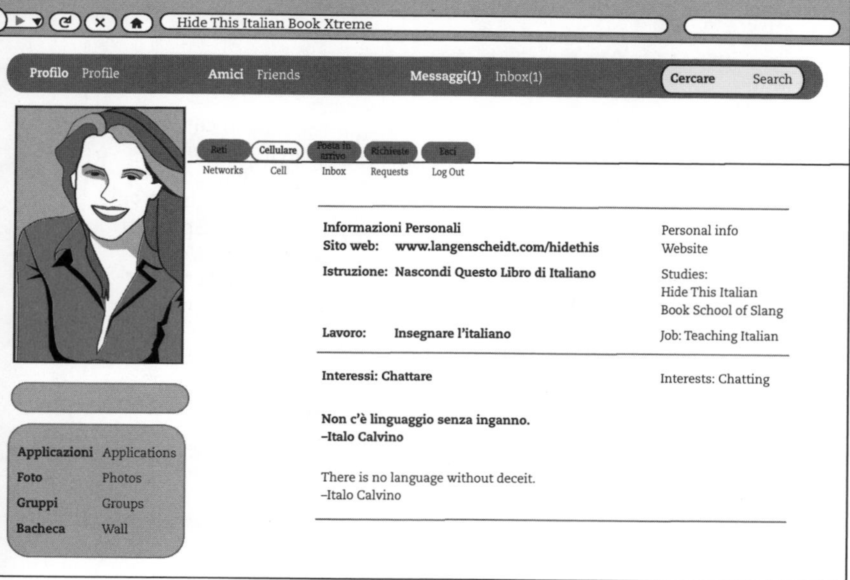

Use It or Lose It!

Before looking at the Word Bytes section, snoop around our profile…

Can you remember three Italian words on the Facebook® page that are similar in English?
What does **profilo** mean?
What does **applicazioni** mean?
What are your **interessi** and what is your **lavoro**?

Word Bytes

applicazioni	applications	**gruppi**	groups
cercare	search	**reti**	networks
esci	close session	**messaggi**	messages
posta in arrivo	inbox	**cellulare**	mobile
istruzione	studies	**lavoro**	job
foto	photos		

Cara Chiara,

Do people from Italy use specific social networking sites?

Saluti,
Signor Profilo

Caro Signor Profilo:

Social networks are definitely cool all over Italy. Most Italian speakers use—you guessed it—MySpace® and Facebook®. But, yes, there are also Italian ones such as *Noemi, Ciaopeople, Italylink* (for Italian Americans and people of Italian heritage) and *Myopencity*.

Some things you can do to give your profile Italian flair is to change the language to Italian and join a language or country-specific MySpace® or Facebook® group. You can also ask your friends to hook you up with Italian-speaking friends—perhaps you'll find that there truly are just six degrees of separation (or maybe fewer).

Un bacio,
Chiara

Online Dating

1 Oggi provo a cercare Stanislao, il mio appuntamento al buio di oggi.

STANISLAO G.
STANISLAO G.

2
Risultati della ricerca
BLOG: I più sexy d'Italia
Raoul Bova, Alessandro Nesta, Riccardo Scamarcio
STANISLAO G.
Wikipedia
Risultati: Stanislao G. Data nascita, 20 luglio 1987
Blogger italiani
Cercasi STANISLAO disperatamente.
Blogga o muori
Non posso vivere senza STANISLAO.
FIGOBLOG
Incontra sexy STANISLAO.

...DING DONG

3 Uau! È qui!

4 Ciao Natalia, sono Stanislao.

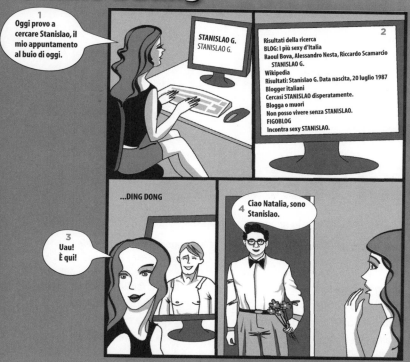

1 I'm going to search Stanislao, my blind date for today. **2** BLOG: The sexiest men in Italy; Raoul Bova, Alessandro Nesta, Riccardo Scamarcio, STANISLAO G. Wikipedia, Results: Stanislao G., born July 20, 1987. Italian Bloggers, Desperately looking for STANISLAO. Blog or die. I can't live without STANISLAO, COOLBLOG, Meet STANISLAO, the sexy. **3** Wow! He's here! **4** Hello, Natalia, I'm Stanislao.

Word Bytes

bloggare	to blog
il/la blogger	blogger
bloggare è il meglio	blogging is the best
leggere blog	to read blogs
le ricerche	searches

Know-it-all/il Saputello

When typing or texting in Italian, sometimes accented letters may be replaced by empty boxes or strange symbols. That means the site you are using does not support the accented letters. To solve the problem, just leave out the accents. People will understand.

Use It or Lose It!

Connect the phrases at your highest speed.

1. to blog	a. **blogger**
2. blogger	b. **leggere blog**
3. to read blogs	c. **bloggare**
4. blogging is the best	d. **bloggare è il meglio**

1. c; 2. a; 3. b; 4. d

All That Slang

Do you YouTube™? Go ahead—in Italian.

Devi vedere questo video su YouTube™.	Check out this YouTube™ video. *Of course, Italian speakers use YouTube™ too!*
Hai un account su YouTube™?	Do you have a YouTube™ account?
Questi sono i video più visti…	These are the most viewed videos…
Come si fa a caricare un video?	How do I upload a video?
Questo video spacca! Dagli cinque stelle.	This video rocks! Give it five stars.
Questo video fa schifo! Dagli una stella.	This video sucks! Give it one star.
Condividi questo video.	Share this video.
Vuoi lasciare un commento?	Would you like to comment?

Word Bytes

Ricerca tutti i video	Search all videos
Ricerca video visualizzabili su Google™	Search videos playable on Google™
I più discussi sui blog	Most blogged
I più condivisi	Most shared
I più visti	Most viewed
Video in ascesa	Movers & Shakers
Video consigliati	Recommended videos
Esplora altri video	Explore more videos

Use It or Lose It!

Choose the correct phrase to answer each question.

1. If you want to tell your friend she must see an awesome video you say:
   a. **Devi vedere questo video su YouTube™.**
   b. **Questi sono i video più visti...**
2. If you want to ask your newest friend if he has a YouTube™ account you say:
   a. **Come si fa a caricare un video?**
   b. **Hai un account su YouTube™?**
3. If you want to pass good judgement on a video you say:
   a. **Questo video spacca! Dagli cinque stelle.**
   b. **Questo video fa schifo! Dagli una stella.**
4. If you want to pass bad judgement on a video you say:
   a. **Questo video spacca! Dagli cinque stelle.**
   b. **Questo video fa schifo! Dagli una stella.**
5. If a video is too cool to keep to yourself, you say:
   a. **Condividi questo video.**
   b. **Vuoi lasciare un commento?**

1. a; 2. b; 3. a; 4. b; 5. a

Know-it-all/il Saputello

Though YouTube™'s interface is in English, you can specify your country content preference by clicking on "Worldwide" and then on Italy. So, as you search on YouTube™, you'll see what videos Italian speakers are watching right now, their favorite videos, etc. Many of the videos selected will be in Italian, so you'll have the added bonus of getting immediate access to contemporary Italian language and visuals.

Google Video™ does interface in Italian; go to video.google.it to immerse yourself in the Italian world of online videos.

A-List

Cool and helpful websites for the tech-savvy Italian speaker...

www.wordreference.com
multilingual dictionary with user forums to discuss words, slang, etc.

www.filmscoop.it
Italian and international movies with reviews and comments

www.lastfm.it
get info about music concerts in Italy, and discover many great bands

www.daveblog.net
a great blog to learn about the world of Italian media

www.stupidexe.com
games, videos and more in Italian and English

www.libero.it
internet search engine and mail provider

www.2night.it
news about venues and events in major Italian cities

Know-it-all/il Saputello

Master Italian technology terms by changing your profile's language and internet settings/preferences to Italian. Also, when searching online, try it.yahoo.com (Yahoo® Italy), or www.google.it (Google® in Italian).

You can also change your computer's default language from English to Italian. This can usually be done through the Preferences feature. If you wish to go back to English, look for ***Preferenze>Lingue>Inglese****.*

Mixed Up

Who hasn't had an embarrassing e-mail mix up like Marina? Fill in the terms to find out what happens...

a. term for webpage
b. place
c. body part
d. adjective
e. person (relation)
f. one word text message

Marina was checking her ________________ (a) at the ________________ (b). Suddenly, she fell and *ha fatto clic* on the wrong keys. Her entire contact list received a nasty message along with a picture of her ________________ (c). In a few minutes, many people answered. Most of them were ________________ (d), including her ________________ (e), who said she was a ________________ (f).

Are you internet savvy, *in italiano?*

1. How many *profili* do you have?
- **a.** I have two, my left and my right.
- **b.** I have two, but I mostly use one.
- **c.** Three that I use and three that I don't.

2. *Un virus* is:
- **a.** a reason to miss a day of school or work.
- **b.** why you avoid *le catene* on your email.
- **c.** the work of hackers (maybe your own)!

3. Your *contratto internet* is:
- **a.** something the phone company charges me for.
- **b.** DSL.
- **c.** *wireless a banda larga* (wireless broadband).

4. RAM is:
- **a.** an uncastrated male sheep.
- **b.** something you like to upgrade to keep more stuff on your computer.
- **c.** Random Access Memory or, in Italian, *memoria ad accesso casuale*.

5. *Scaricare* means:
- **a.** to unload the car.
- **b.** to watch a video.
- **c.** to download.

6. You use your *posta elettronica*:
- **a.** once a week.
- **b.** for work and some jokes, daily.
- **c.** every five seconds.

Mainly As

You still don't get what all the fuss is about the internet (boy, are you missing out)...

Mainly Bs

You are a well-rounded internet user.

Mainly Cs

You are an expert, *un maniaco di internet*♂/*una maniaca di internet*♀.

Gadgets

chapter 6

Get info on:

- names for trendy gadgets
- talking about your cool electronic stuff
- working your cell phone and MP3 player in Italian

E-junk

1 Ecco fatto! Ho inventato l'e-coltellino svizzero!
2 Cosa? Come no...
3 Guarda, c'è cellulare, segreteria, SMS, Bluetooth™, lettore DVD e video, MP3, telecamera digitale, mail, tastiera e mouse...
4 Francesco, è esattamente come un iPhone® o un Blackberry®, solo che è enorme e scomodo.
5 Ma il mio ha anche la stampante...e servono solo 20 pile stilo AA.

1 I made it! I invented the e-Swiss Army Knife! **2** What? Yeah right... **3** Look, it has a cell phone with voice mail, text messaging, Bluetooth™, video and DVD player, MP3 player, digital camera, e-mail, keyboard and mouse... **4** Francesco, that's the same thing as an iPhone® or a Blackberry®, but gigantic and inconvenient. **5** But mine prints... and it only uses 20 AA batteries.

Word Bytes

il computer, il PC computer

il portatile
laptop

la tastiera keyboard

il mouse
mouse

la stampante
printer

il lettore video, DVD e Blu-ray
video, DVD and Blu-ray player
Lettore means player.

la fotocamera digitale
digital camera
An old-fashioned camera is a *macchina fotografica.*

il telefonino, il cellulare
cell phone

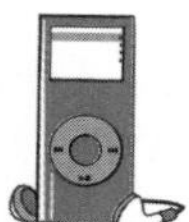

l'MP3, il lettore MP3
MP3 player

le cuffie
headphones

le casse
speakers

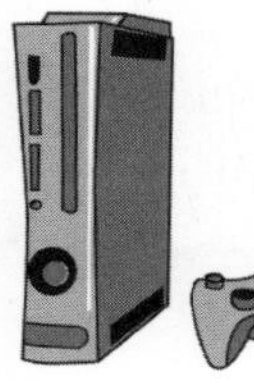

la console
Wii™, Playstation®, Xbox™, etc.

lo schermo
screen

Use It or Lose It!

Can you find these gadgets in this *crucipuzzle*?

1. console **3. pc** **5. telefonino** **7. stampante**
2. computer **4. schermo** **6. cuffie** **8. tastiera**

T O N V I D E O J U E O S I F O S Y
C O N S O L E I D E O J U O R E C M
A U O I F O N C O M P U T E R O H A
M P F R A O N I N O F E L E T A E O
L A A F D I S T A M P A N T E A R K
E N A M I O R D E N A D O R D E M L
T A S T I E R A O V I L T O N M O U
A E O J U I I F O N M P C E S O R A

Cara Chiara,
Are there Italian terms for gadgets like the iPod®?

Saluti,
E-talian

Caro E-talian,
Many of the gadgets out there retain their English name in Italian. There is one difference, though—the pronunciation of the word.

ENGLISH GADGET	ITALIAN PRONUNCIATION
iPod®	eye-podd, accent is on eye, and emphasize the d
iPhone®	eye-fohn
MP3	ehm-meh-py-treh
Blackberry®	just like in English, but emphasize the double r
Palm Pilot®	pahlm pih-loht

I hope this guide helps you.

Chiara

Dialogue: When Gadgets Go Wrong

Emiliano calls Raffaella to talk about a cool gadget, but the reception is bad. Let's see how Raffaella reacts.

EMILIANO:	**Pronto? C'è Raffaella per favore?**	Hello? Is Raffaella there, please?
RAFFAELLA:	**Sì, pronto? Dimmi in fretta però, perché non prende bene.**	Yes, hello? Talk to me quicky, the signal is bad.
EMILIANO:	**Ciao Raffaé, come va?**	Hey Raffaé, how's it going?
RAFFAELLA:	**Bene, allora, che c'è?**	OK, so what's up then?
EMILIANO:	**Sì, Raffaé, sono Emi. Volevo dirti che è arrivato il nuovo cellulare che volevi, con la videocamera, foto e internet integrati, ce l'ho qui.**	Yes, Raffaé, it's Emi. I wanted to tell you that the new cell you wanted with camera, video and integrated internet has arrived, I've got it here.
RAFFAELLA:	**Pronto? Pronto? Non sento, sta cadendo la linea.**	Hello? hello? I can't hear you, the signal is bad.
EMILIANO:	**Cazzo Raffaella, mi senti?** (to himself) **Questo Bluetooth™ fa schifo.**	Damn it, Raffaella, can you hear me? This Bluetooth™ sucks.
RAFFAELLA:	**Ah! Lascia un messaggio dopo il "bip".**	Ha! Leave a message after the beep.
SEGRETERIA:	**BIP**	BEEP
EMILIANO:	**Raffaé, ci sentiamo su Skype™. E cambia questo cazzo di messaggio per favore…**	Raffaé, let's talk on Skype™; and please change that damn voice message…

Use It or Lose It!

Can you pass the polygraph? Write *vero* if the sentence is true or *falso* if it's false.

1. Raffaella answered the phone, but the connection was bad.
2. Raffaella is in a hurry because the connection is bad.
3. Emiliano wants to show Raffaella the latest and coolest phone, the one she wanted.

1. *falso*, Raffaella never answered the phone, it was her voicemail message; 2. *falso*; 3. *vero*

Word Bytes

For your cell phone…

schermo
screen
menù
menu
tastiera
key pad
tasto
key

l'altoparlante	speaker phone	**la rubrica**	contacts
chiamare	to call	**la segreteria**	voice mail
la chiamata persa	missed call	**seleziona**	select
le chiamate effettuate	dialed calls	**silenzioso**	silent
le chiamate ricevute	received calls	**gli strumenti**	tools
esci	end/exit	**la suoneria**	ringtone
le impostazioni	settings	**termina chiamata**	end call
indietro	back	**vai a**	go to
invia	send	**la vibrazione**	vibrate
muto	mute	**visualizza**	view

Know-it-all/il Saputello

Change your phone to Italian: menu>settings>language>Italian. Now, send a text message: **menù>messaggi>scrivi messaggio**. To go back to English: **menù>impostazioni>telefono>lingua>**English. (May vary by phone.)

Quiz What should you do to…

1. send a text message to your BF from your *cellulare*? Click:
   a. *menù>messaggi>scrivi messaggio*
   b. *menù>messaggi>messaggi ricevuti*

2. call your friend Anna? Go to:
   a. *rubrica>Anna>chiama*
   b. *rubrica>Anna>opzioni*

3. turn your phone from ring to vibrate? Click:
   a. *impostazioni>esci>seleziona*
   b. *impostazioni>toni>vibrazione*

1. a; 2. a; 3. b

Word Bytes

For your MP3 player…

gli album	albums
gli artisti	artists
gli audiolibri	audiobooks
gli autori	authors
avanti	forward
il blocco	block
i brani casuali	shuffle songs
i brani	songs
il calendario	calendar
casuale	shuffle
i compositori	artists
i contatti	contacts
il cronometro	stopwatch
i film	movies
le foto	pictures, photos
i generi	genres
la ghiera	click wheel
i giochi	games
le impostazioni	settings
le impostazioni video	video settings
indietro	reverse
menù	menu
la musica	music
le note	notes
l'orologio	clock
la pausa	pause
play	play
le playlist	playlist
i podcast	podcasts
i programmi TV	TV shows
la ricerca	search
seleziona	menu button
i video	video
i video podcast	video podcasts
i videoclip	music videos
volume	volume

Know-it-all/il Saputello

Turn your MP3 player to Italian. Just go to settings>language>Italian. To turn it back to English go to ***impostazioni>lingua****>English.*

All That Slang

Gadgets are great, except when they stop working... Here are a few lines you might need when technology works, or when it fails.

Si è rotto il computer.	The computer broke.
Devo portare il computer da un tecnico.	I have to take the computer to tech support.
C'è un virus nel computer.	The computer has a virus.
Non mi piacciono né la tastiera ergonomica né il mouse senza fili.	I don't like the ergonomic keyboard and wireless mouse.
Il mio cellulare non funziona bene.	My cell's not working well.
Il telefono non prende in questa zona.	The phone has no service in this area.
Prende poco.	I have barely any bars.
Devo ricaricare la batteria del cellulare.	I need to recharge the cell's battery.
Cazzo, non ho più batteria.	Damn it, the battery is dead.
Scusa, è caduta la linea.	Sorry, I lost the signal.
Ha ignorato la mia chiamata.	He/She ignored my phone call.
Mi ha risposto la voicemail.	The call went straight to voicemail.
Devo controllare la voicemail il prima possibile.	I need to check my voicemail ASAP.
Metto l'altoparlante.	I'll put the speakerphone on.
Questo telefono è un fossile.	This phone is a fossil.
Mi presti il cellulare? Devo fare una chiamata.	Can I borrow your cell? I need to make a call.
Mando questa mail dal telefonino.	I'll send this e-mail from my cell.
Devo resettare l'iPod®.	I have to reset my iPod®.
Devo sincronizzare l'iPod®.	I have to sync the iPod®.
L'iPod® di merda si è bloccato.	Shit, my iPod® is frozen.
Ho scaricato quella canzone sul computer.	I downloaded that song to my computer.

Quiz Are you a gadget freak?

1. Your favorite electronic device is:
 a. you can't choose—you couldn't live without any of them.
 b. you can't decide between your *cellulare*, your iPod® or your *computer*.
 c. your *microonde*.

2. Your *cellulare* is:
 a. a Blackberry® or an iPhone®—you need to be *connesso* at all times.
 b. a cool one with *foto e videocamera integrate*.
 c. standard issue—it came free with the contract.

3. You keep your *calendario*:
 a. on your Blackberry®, otherwise you couldn't function.
 b. on your computer's e-calendar.
 c. hanging on your wall...duh. You got it from Mom last year.

4. Your *musica* listening schedule is:
 a. 24/7. You're always *connesso* to your iPod®, your *cellulare* or your *computer*.
 b. occasional. You like to do your chores while listening to your iPod®.
 c. infrequent. You have a *lettore CD* at home.

Mainly As
You're a child of the digital age. You may forget that there is a whole (physical) world outside of your computer room...

Mainly Bs
You are a well-balanced *ragazzo*♂/*ragazza*♀. You use your gadgets to your advantage, but you still need someone to help fix them when they fail.

Mainly Cs
You must have been born in the dark ages. Why not take advantage of the digital age and get tech savvy?!

Mixed Up

Write a list of spicy Italian words you've picked up so far. Then insert them in the text. What happens to Luca?

a. name of gadget b. noun c. infinitive verb d. place

Luca broke his ____________ (a) and decided to fix it using his ____________ (b). Of course it didn't work. Luca decided he would instead ____________ (c) the thing. That didn't work either. "What can I do now?" he thought. Maybe he would just take the thing chapter 7

Style

Get info on:

- Italian fashion
- decorating your space like a real Italian

In a Dressing Room

Bella... Quei pantaloni non mi piacciono mica, ti si vede il culo... Però la scollatura della camicetta ti sta benissimo!
Cutie... I don't like those pants, your ass is showing... But the cleavage on that blouse is great on you!

Che costume ti piace di più?
Which bathing suit looks better?
Quello intero non mi piace per niente. Bella, con il fisico che hai, devi prenderti il bikini!
I don't like the one-piece at all. Cutie, with a body like yours, you should get the bikini!

Guarda, questo smoking ti sta una meraviglia... ma ti servirebbe una maglietta sotto.
Look, this tux looks great on you... but you need an undershirt.

Word Bytes

l'abito	dress
gli accessori	accessories
la biancheria	underwear
i boxer	boxer shorts
i calzini	socks
il camerino	dressing room
la camicetta	blouse
la camicia	shirt
il cappotto, la giacca	coat
la cintura	belt
il completo	suit
il costume (da bagno)	bathing suit
la cravatta	tie
la giacchetta	jacket
la gonna	skirt
la maglietta	undershirt
le mutandine	panties
gli occhiali da sole	sunglasses
l'orologio	watch
i pantaloni	pants
il pullover	sweater
il reggiseno	bra
le scarpe	shoes
le scarpe coi tacchi	high heels
la scollatura	cleavage
lo smoking	tux
gli stivali	boots
la t-shirt	T-shirt
il vestito	outfit

Use It or Lose It!

In what order do you put on your clothes (assuming you're NOT a superhero)? Put each list of clothes in the right order.

1. **pullover, t-shirt, reggiseno**
2. **cintura, pantaloni, mutande**
3. **cravatta, giacchetta, canottiera, camicia**

1. reggiseno, t-shirt, pullover
2. mutande, pantaloni, cintura
3. canottiera, camicia, cravatta, giacca hetta

All That Slang

Sta bene/male.	It looks good/ugly.
Quei pantaloni sono molto chic.	Those pants are very chic.
Quella gonna è sexy.	That skirt is sexy.
Questa camicia è elegante.	This shirt is elegant.
Quelle scarpe sono orrende, non stanno bene con il vestito.	Those shoes are horrible; they don't look good with that dress.
Quei jeans ti stanno troppo stretti.	Those jeans are too tight on you.
È troppo scollata ♀.	There's too much cleavage.
La gonna è troppo corta, ti si vede il culo.	The skirt is too short; it doesn't cover your butt.
Quella camicetta è trasparente.	That blouse is see-through.
Ti si vede tutto.	You can see everything.
Che ridicolo ♂/ridicola ♀!	He/She looks ridiculous!
Cosa si è messo ♂/messa ♀?	What is he/she wearing?
Ma ti sei guardato ♂/guardata ♀ allo specchio?	Did you look in the mirror?
Quella camicia non sta bene con quei pantaloni.	That shirt doesn't go with those pants.
Che ti è saltato in mente?	What were you thinking?
Tirati su i pantaloni, ti si vede il culo.	Pull up your pants, your ass is showing.
Hai la patta aperta.	Your fly is down.

Forse potresti metterti qualcos'altro.

Maybe you could put on something else.

Ti sta proprio bene!

It looks really good on you!

Quelle scarpe sono splendide!

Those shoes are spectacular!

Quel vestito fa veramente schifo. 💣

That dress really sucks.

Cazzo, che bello quel vestito! 💣

Fuck, that dress is great!

Con quello schifo di scarpe sembri un pezzente.

You look like a bum with those crappy shoes.

Quiz Cosa ti metti?

Do you know what to wear in order to *stare una meraviglia?*

Che ti metti per…?
What do you wear to…?

1. *andare a un colloquio di lavoro* (a work interview):
  a. *jeans, t-shirt, giacchetta*
  b. *camicetta/camicia, pantaloni*
  c. *un abito firmato* (designer suit/dress)—you'd better get the job if you want to be able to pay for it

2. *andare a un gran galà* (a gala):
  a. *jeans, t-shirt*
  b. *vestito, cravatta*
  c. *un abito da sera con scarpe coi tacchi*

3. *andare a ballare* (a dance club):
  a. *t-shirt, pantaloni*
  b. *una minigonna, scarpe coi tacchi*
  c. *un vestito alla* Sex and the City

4. *andare in campeggio* (go camping):
  a. *una giacchetta o un abito*
  b. *pantaloni corti, t-shirt*
  c. *vestito nuovo*, everything name brand of course, designer *trekking* (hiking boots) and expensive *occhiali da sole*

5. *andare al centro commerciale* (the mall):
  a. *costume, scarpe coi tacchi*
  b. *jeans, camicia/camicetta*
  c. *jeans firmati, camicetta con strass* (bling) and *scarpe coi tacchi*

Mostly As
You have no idea of what is appropriate. Still, you feel comfortable in your clothes.

Mostly Bs
You dress well, but you're not gonna be on the cover of a magazine any time soon.

Mostly Cs
You really know your fashion! But be careful, you might overdo it sometimes, not to mention the hole your dressing habits leave in your pockets.

Use It or Lose It!

The paparazzi are working the Italian Xtreme Music Awards. You are the Fashion Police. What will you say about each artist? Choose from the expressions below. Extra! See if you can find the biggest fashion faux pas. Here's a hint: it isn't one of the artists.

a. **Quei pantaloni ti stanno grandi.**
b. **Quelle scarpe sono orrende, non stanno bene con il vestito.**
c. **Che ridicola!**
d. **Ma ti sei guardato♂/guardata♀ allo specchio?**
e. **La gonna è troppo corta, ti si vede il culo.**
f. **È troppo scollata.**

And there's only one thing to say about that photographer on the left, whose huge crack is visible:

Ti si vede il culo!

1. b; 2. d; 3. e; 4. a; 5. f; 6. c

Il Designer

1
Ciao, e benvenuti a Scambio Casa. In questa puntata, le sorelle Del Favero si scambiano di casa e le ri-arredano secondo i propri gusti. Vediamo che pensano delle camere.

Salotto e cucina di Michela: Prima
Michela's living room and kitchen: Before

Salotto e cucina di Michela: Dopo
Michela's living room and kitchen: After
2
È stupendo quel che hai fatto con l'appartamento. Gli accessori della cucina sono i migliori in circolazione. Mi piace tutto! I mobili sono comodi. Mi affascinano gli accostamenti di colore.
3
Ho uno stile eclettico e mi sono ispirata alla spiaggia.

Camera da letto di Lisa: Prima
Lisa's Room: Before

Camera di Lisa: Dopo
Lisa's Room: After
4
C'è un quadro con ritratto di famiglia e uno specchio sul soffitto.
5
Che cattivo gusto. Non mi piace… mi piaceva di più prima.
6
Il letto almeno è bello.

1 Hello, this is Trading Interiors. In this episode the Del Favero sisters have traded houses and re-designed them to their taste. Let's see what they think about their rooms. **2** I love what you have done with the apartment. The kitchen appliances are the newest models. I love everything! The furniture is comfortable. I love the color combination. **3** My style is eclectic and my inspiration was the beach. **4** There is a painting with a portrait of your family and a mirror on the ceiling. **5** How tacky. I don't like it… I want my house like before. **6** At least the bed is pretty.

Use It or Lose It!

Can you pass the polygraph? Write *vero* if it's true and *falso* if it's false.

1. Michela hates her *salotto.*
2. Lisa adores her *camera.*
3. There is a *candeliere* in Michela's room.
4. The *cucina* is the place where you cook.

1. falso; 2. falso; 3. falso; 4. vero

Word Bytes

Some items and phrases you might have seen on *Scambio Casa...*

l'accostamento di colore	color combination
l'appartamento	apartment
l'armadio	closet
arredare	to design
l'arte	art
la camera, la stanza	room
la camera da letto	bedroom
le candele	candles
il candeliere	chandelier
la casa	house
Che cattivo gusto!	How tacky!
il comodino	night table
il cuscino	pillow
il divano	sofa
gli elettrodomestici	household appliances
la finestra	window
il fornello	stove top
il forno	oven
il frigo, il frigorifero	refrigerator
il gusto	taste
Il mio stile è... minimalista/ eclettico/ moderno/ classico.	My style is... minimalist/ eclectic/ modern/ classic.
l'ispirazione	inspiration
la lampada	lamp
il lavello	(kitchen) sink
il legno/in legno	wood/wooden
la libreria	bookcase
il microonde	microwave
i mobili	furniture
la parete/il muro	wall (inner/outer)
la piscina	swimming pool
la porta	door
il quadro	painting
il ritratto	portrait
il salotto	living room
la sedia	chair
lo specchio	mirror
il tavolino	coffee table
il tavolo	table
le tendine	curtains
il ventilatore	fan

Use It or Lose It!

What's up with *la camera di Lisa*? ID each hideous item in Italian.

1. bed
2. pillow
3. curtain
4. window
5. mirror
6. fan
7. painting

1. letto; 2. cuscino; 3.tendine; 4. finestra; 5. specchio; 6. ventilatore; 7. quadro

Quiz *Come starebbe meglio?*

What would look better?

1. *in un salotto rosso:*
  a. *divano blu* with polka-dots
  b. *divano marrone scuro*

2. *in camera da letto:*
  a. *un lavandino*
  b. *un comodino*

3. *nel patio:*
  a. *delle tendine*
  b. *una piscina*

4. *in cucina:*
  a. *un letto in legno*
  b. *delle superfici di marmo*

Mostly As: *Hai cattivo gusto.*
Please hire a designer; doing it yourself could be detrimental to your home.

Mostly Bs: *Hai buon gusto.*
Are you a *stilista d'interni,* a designer, or just naturally savvy with design?

Word Bytes

il bianco	white	**il marrone**	brown	**il rosso**	red
il blu	blue	**il nero**	black	**il verde**	green
il giallo	yellow	**il rosa**	pink	**il viola**	purple

What do ya think of those colors? Put one of these after a color to describe it.

brillante	bright	**pastello**	pastel

Health

Get info on:

- relaxation: mind and body
- gross bodily functions
- STDs and other issues

All That Slang

Stressed out? Get it off your chest.

Ho il torcicollo.	I have a stiff neck.
Dovresti fare stretching e rilassarti.	You should do some stretching and relax.
Il lavoro e l'università/la scuola mi fanno impazzire.	Work and college/school are driving me crazy. *__La scuola__ is school from elementary to high school.*
Sono stressato da morire.	I'm dying of stress.
Ti va di fare yoga?	Do you want to do yoga?
Non sono molto sciolto.	I'm not very flexible.
Andiamo in palestra?	Should we go to the gym?
Non ti preoccupare, andrà tutto bene!	Don't worry, everything will be OK!
Oh, ti vedo teso♂/tesa♀.	Wow, you look tense.
Rilassati e sii felice.	Relax, be happy.
Amore, mettiti comodo♂/comoda♀, ti faccio un massaggio dalla testa ai piedi.	My love, get comfortable; I'm going to give you a head-to-toe massage.
Dovresti rilassarti, ti verranno le rughe per lo stress.	You should relax; stress gives you wrinkles.

Use It or Lose It!

Rilassati! Just follow this *esercizio di rilassamento* and feel your tensions melt. For xtreme relaxation, see if you can follow the audio instructions without peeking at the book.

Trova una posizione comoda:	Look for a comfortable position:
Siediti o stenditi, e rilassati.	Sit down or lie down, and relax.
Per prima cosa, respira profondamente.	First, take a deep breath.
Inspira, trattieni il fiato, e espira.	Inhale, hold your breath and exhale.
Le spalle e il collo sono già più rilassati.	Your shoulders and neck are not tense.
Rilassa gli occhi e la bocca.	Relax your eyes and mouth.
Sei felice.	You are happy.
Non smettere di respirare.	Don't stop breathing.
Ora, alzati.	Now stand up.
Ripeti questo esercizio per tre volte.	Repeat the exercise three times.

Use It or Lose It!

Stai morendo dallo stress? Is stress killing you? These people are hurting too. Join each situation with the phrase that describes it.

1. Luigi has too much homework. He says…
2. Oli cannot reach his toes during yoga. He says…
3. Rita is stressing about everything. Your obligation as a friend is to warn her…
4. What you wish your boyfriend or girlfriend would say to you after a long day…
5. Franco did not do the relaxation exercises for his *collo*. Now he is complaining…
6. You notice your friend is too stressed. You suggest…

a. **Ho il torcicollo.**
b. **L'università mi fa impazzire.**
c. **Vuoi fare yoga?**
d. **Non sono molto sciolto.**
e. **Dovresti rilassarti, ti verranno le rughe per lo stress.**
f. **Amore, mettiti comodo♂/comoda♀ che ti faccio un massaggio dalla testa ai piedi.**

1. b; 2. d; 3. e; 4. f; 5. a; 6. c.

All That Slang

Health isn't just about relaxation and stress. Here's the grosser side of taking care of your body.

Mi sto cacando/pisciando sotto.	I'm going to shit/pee myself. *Use this one when you really need a bathroom. Note that these can also mean "I'm scared shitless".*
Ho la sciolta. Dov'è il bagno?	I have the runs. Where's the bathroom?
Cazzo, è finita la carta igienica! 💣	Shit, there's no TP!
Aiuto! Chi ha scoreggiato?	Yuck! Who farted?
Sono pieno♂/piena♀ di brufoli.	My face is full of pimples.
Mi cola il naso.	I've got snot coming out of my nose.
Ha fatto uno scaracchio enorme.	He/She spit a big loogey.
Ho un raffreddore terribile.	I have a terrible cold.
Sara ha vomitato anche l'anima.	Sara puked her guts out. *Literally, Sara vomited her soul out.*
Dopo la sbronza di ieri ho dei postumi tremendi.	Last night's bender gave me a huge hangover.
Mi fa male la pancia/la schiena/la testa. Mi sento uno schifo.	My tummy/back/head hurts. I feel like garbage.

And for those special, below-the-belt, health situations:

Dove sta la pillola/stanno i gommini?	Where are the birth control pills/condoms?
Quel♂/Quella♀ deficiente mi ha attaccato le piattole.	That idiot gave me crabs.
Detesto le malattie veneree.	I hate STDs. *The term for STDs is **MST, malattie sessualmente trasmissibili**. Note: In spoken Italian, **MST** would not be used.*

Know-it-all/il Saputello

*When you say **Lui♂/Lei♀ ha bevuto** you're saying that a person has drunk too much. If you say **Lui♂/Lei♀ beve,** you're saying someone is a lush or an alcoholic.*

Know-it-all/il Saputello

When somebody sneezes, you should be polite and say **salute** (bless you). You say the same thing when you make a toast; it's like saying "to your health".

Quiz What would you say when...?

1. you're out of TP:
 a. *Cazzo, è finita la carta igienica!*
 b. Nothing, you just use the receipt from your last purchase.
 c. *Mi sto cacando sotto!*

2. someone sneezes:
 a. *Salute!*
 b. Cheers!
 c. *Cazzo!*

3. someone farts:
 a. *Aiuto! Chi ha scorreggiato?*
 b. What is that funky smell?
 c. *Quel/quella deficiente mi ha attaccato le piattole.*

4. your head aches, your body is producing excessive amounts of snot and you're coughing and sneezing like crazy:
 a. *Ho un raffreddore terribile.*
 b. I feel like crap.
 c. *Ho bevuto.*

5. you make a pit stop at the pharmacy before an X-rated date:
 a. *Dove sono gli anticoncezionali?*
 b. Can I get an extra large condom?
 c. *Ho dei postumi tremendi.*

Mostly As
Good for you, you really know your slang!

Mostly Bs
You really should try to speak more Italian; you never know how much you've learned until you try it.

Mostly Cs
You have no idea what's going on around in any language. Careful! You might catch something nasty.

Go Green

chapter 9

Get info on:

- being green, Italian style

Essere ecologista

Grazie, non mi serve, ho la mia.
Thanks, neither, I brought my own.
Le do una borsa di plastica o di carta?
Do you want paper or plastic bags?
Patatina, l'organico puzza da morire.
Babe, that compost stinks too much.
Sì, sì, è uno schifo.
Yeah, it's disgusting.
Odio i vestiti usati! Specie i vestiti di mia sorella.
I hate reusing! Especially my sister's clothes.
Dillo a me! Era finita la carta igienica...
Tell me about it! There was no TP...
Bleah! E manco c'è l'acqua calda...
Yuck! Plus there's no hot water...

All That Slang

Hey, *ecologista*, here's the lingo that you've gotta know…

Mi dai un passaggio sulla tua ibrida? — Can you give me a ride in your hybrid? *In Italian there's no word for carpool, but lately* ***carsharing*** *(pronounced with Italian accent: rolled r and strong g at the end) is becoming popular.*

L'inquinamento ci sta fottendo. — Pollution is fucking us.

C'è troppo smog. — There's too much smog.

Cazzo che caldo, deve essere l'effetto serra. — Damn it's hot! It must be the greenhouse effect.

Merda! Mi sono dimenticato ♂/ dimenticata ♀ la borsa di tela. — Oh crap! I forgot to bring my own shopping bag.

Cristina usa sempre un thermos. — Cristina always uses her thermos.

Davide il caffè lo prende sempre nella sua tazza da viaggio. — Davide gets coffee only in his refillable travel mug.

Use It or Lose It!

Find these *ecologista* words in the *crucipuzzle*. For bonus points, find the one un-green word in there.

riciclare **ridurre** **ecologista** **ambiente** **ibrida** **passaggio**

```
A H E C O L O G I S T A L C M A E G
M K J H S G R O E C O L O R Z S T A
B W S J Y T P A S S A G G I O H T E
I F I M A N N E D H A U R D D C O R
E G T A O X J V L E S S R U E J E O
N E A R F G K T I O V I B R I D A W
T C K T A L V Y R N T L S R C N J O
E I R I C I C L A R E H A E U C V M
```

Your bonus word is smog.

Quiz Sei ecologista?

1. At the end of a meal, you:
   - **a.** wash the dishes by hand, with *sapone eco-compatibile* (eco-friendly soap).
   - **b.** put the dishes in the dishwasher, but wait until it's full to turn it on.
   - **c.** throw everything in the garbage, plates and all. Hey, that's what disposable plates are for!

2. When you go to *il supermercato* (the supermarket) you:
   - **a.** bring your own *borse*.
   - **b.** request *borse di carta*, paper bags, and reuse them later.
   - **c.** get paper bags in plastic bags. It's free, plus you wouldn't want anything to rip or break!

3. When you go on vacation, you:
   - **a.** backpack or enjoy an ecotour—you want to be part of nature!
   - **b.** make sure to turn off the lights and air conditioning in your hotel room when you leave for the day.
   - **c.** live it up—there's no excess you can't handle!

4. You get around:
   - **a.** by *bici* (bike) or *a piedi* (on foot).
   - **b.** *auto ibrida* or public transportation.
   - **c.** SUV—you love that Hummer.

5. When you eat, you:
   - **a.** use silverware, ceramic plates and cloth napkins, then you make an *organico* with the leftovers.
   - **b.** use your own plates, but you always use paper napkins.
   - **c.** use disposable forks and paper plates—doubled so they don't leak.

6. You use your *aria condizionata*:
   - **a.** only if it's more than 100°F. You can handle heat waves with water, cold showers and maybe a fan while you are sleeping.
   - **b.** for sleeping only. You go to the beach or the mall during the day to beat the heat.
   - **c.** *tutto il giorno*, (all day long)! There's a reason why they exist, and you don't mind the electric bill.

Mostly As: *Sei un♂/una♀ ecologista.*
You are green as a tree in *primavera* (spring). If recycling were a religion, you would be the pope. Being green is good—just make sure you're not too smug about it.

Mostly Bs: *Stai diventando ecologista.*
You're trying to be green while maintaining some type of comfort. Keep working, it's worth it.

Mostly Cs: *Sei un♂/una♀ ammazza-alberi.*
Among other things, you are a "tree assassin". You'd better change your ways—the icebergs might just take it personally.

Travel

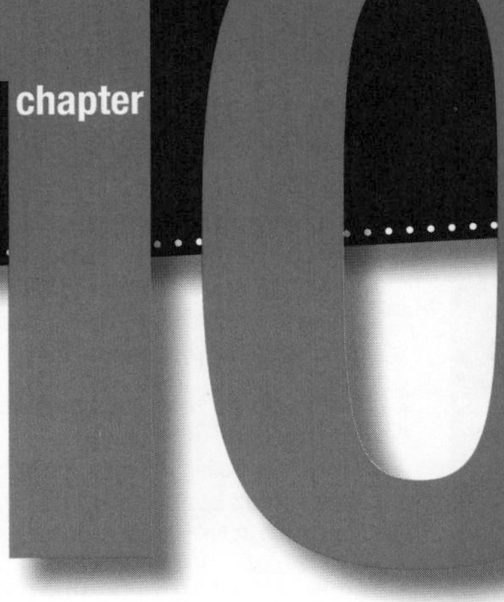
chapter
10

Get info on:

- must-see places
- the cash you need
- hotel lingo
- bar and club lingo
- tasty treats and trendy drinks
- shopping

Le foto delle vacanze

Serena is very forgetful and she's always misplacing things. For example, she just found an SD card from her digital camera with hundreds of pictures from various vacations. Now she's going through the photos and trying to figure out where she was and what she was doing.

Ora mi ricordo! Quando ero in crociera con i miei, prendevo il sole, e poi mi è venuta la nausea!
I remember this well! I went on a cruise with my parents, I tanned out by the pool and I got sick!

Sono andata in Sicilia con mia sorella, stavamo in un boutique hotel e passavamo tutto il giorno in spiaggia. È stato bellissimo!
I went to Sicily with my sister; we stayed in a boutique hotel and spent all day on the beach. It was so nice!

Mi sono piaciuti tantissimo i musei di Firenze quando ci sono andata con la scuola. Non ho ancora visto tutti gli Uffizi.
Oh, I loved the museums in Florence when I went there with my class. I still haven't seen everything there is to see in the Uffizi.

Ero andata a Roma con il mio ragazzo Luca. Stavamo facendo un giro turistico ma ci eravamo persi. A Luca non piace chiedere indicazioni.
I went on a trip to Rome with my boyfriend Luca. We went sightseeing and got lost in the city. Luca doesn't like to ask for directions.

Sono andata a fare la vendemmia in campagna.
I did the vintage in the countryside.

Sono andata zaino in spalla in Sardegna. È stato fighissimo, adoro l'avventura.
I went backpacking in Sardinia. It was awesome—I love adventure.

Sono andata a sciare sulle Alpi con i miei amici. Che freddo!
I went skiing in the Alps with my friends. It was so cold!

Use It or Lose It!

Serena has finally posted all of her vacation pics to her blog and now she needs to add a description to each picture. Can you help her?

a. 

b. 

c. 

d. 

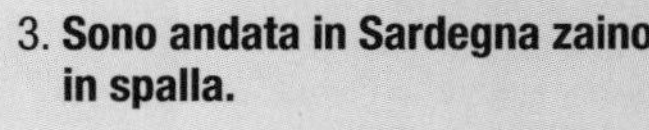

e. 

f. 

g. 

1. **Sono andata a fare la vendemmia in campagna.**
2. **Ero a Roma con il mio ragazzo Luca.**
3. **Sono andata in Sardegna zaino in spalla.**
4. **Ero in crociera con i miei.**
5. **Sono andata agli Uffizi con la scuola.**
6. **Sono andata a sciare sulle Alpi con i miei amici.**
7. **In Sicilia stavo in un boutique hotel con mia sorella.**

1. e; 2. d; 3. f; 4. a; 5. c; 6. g; 7. b

Are you a nice tourist or a naughty one?

andare in spiaggia, go to the beach

bere qualcosa in un locale del posto, get a drink in a local bar

meet *qualcuno*, someone, at a club

vedere un film, watch a movie

talk to a local in his or her language

andare in una spiaggia nudista, go to a nudist beach

ubriacarsi, get drunk, in *un locale del posto*

go back to your hotel room with *qualcuno* you just met

guardare, watch, *un peep show* (pronounced with Italian accent: *pyp shoh*)

insult a local in his or her language

A-List

Top 15 things to do in Italy…

1. See Michelangelo's *Cappella Sistina* and *San Pietro* in Rome.
2. Take a *gondola* ride in Venice.
3. Visit *Pompei* ruins, near Naples, and hike *il Vesuvio*, a volcano.
4. Climb *Torre degli Asinelli* in Bologna.
5. Enjoy *il Parco Nazionale dello Stelvio*, with its 400,000 hectares of protected nature.
6. Snorkel in *Isole Eolie*, Sicily.
7. Go to *Piazza del Campo* to watch *Il Palio di Siena*, the famous horse race.
8. Eat *ossobuco alla Milanese* (veal braised in white wine and tomatoes) with a glass of *vino* in Milan.
9. Go to the opera at the *Arena di Verona*.
10. Hike the *Alpi*.
11. Throw a *monetina* (small coin) into the *Fontana di Trevi* in Rome.
12. Go to *Repubblica di San Marino* and enjoy the hill-top views.
13. Participate in la *battaglia delle arance*, the orange-throwing festival in Ivrea, during *Carnevale*.
14. Go clubbing in *Costa Smeralda*, Sardinia, while enjoying its *mare* and *spiagge*.
15. Go to *Carnevale di Venezia* and wear a *maschera*, mask.

Use It or Lose It!

Camilla did the Xtreme vacation tour. Name the can't-miss experience in each picture from Camilla's vacation album.

1.

2.

3.

4.

5.

1. Alpi
2. Carnevale di Venezia
3. Pompei
4. Fontana di Trevi
5. Repubblica di San Marino

Dialogue: Il Sig. Rossi arrives at Hotel V

Quante domande che fa questo tipo!
This dude has so many questions!
Le auguro un buon soggiorno!
I hope you enjoy your stay!

Hotel V is *un hotel boutique* in the imaginary city of Pomaretto Marittima. Check out its awesome amenities. Mr. Rossi, an annoying first-time client, is checking in.

ELISA:	**Benvenuto Sig. Rossi. La sua camera è la Warhol, con vista sul mare.**	Welcome Mr. Rossi. Your room is the Warhol, with an ocean view.
SIG. ROSSI:	**Grazie. Ehi, Elisa, c'è una connessione internet wireless in camera?**	Thanks. Hey, Elisa, is there wireless internet in the room?
ELISA:	**Si, in tutto l'hotel. Ci sono anche videogiochi e video gratis.**	Yes, everywhere in the hotel. There are also free video games and videos.
SIG. ROSSI:	**Che altri servizi offrite?**	What other amenities are there?
ELISA:	**Molti. C'è un bar, un ristorante con specialità di pesce, un centro benessere, una piscina, una sala riunioni, servizio bar con snack inclusi, servizio parcheggio per i clienti, noleggio biciclette e cellulari e molte altre cosucce. Ecco un depliant con tutte le informazioni.**	A lot. We have a bar, seafood restaurant, spa, pool, business center, juice bar with complementary snacks, valet service and parking for guests, bike and cell phone rentals and a lot of other little things. Here's a brochure with all the info.
SIG. ROSSI:	**Posso portar via lo shampoo dell'hotel?**	Can I take the hotel's shampoo?
ELISA:	**Certo.**	Of course.
SIG. ROSSI:	**Grande, che hotel figo!**	Wow, what a cool hotel!
SIG. ROSSI:	**Un'ultima cosa, dov'è l'ascensore?**	One last thing—where's the elevator?
ELISA:	**Uhm, non c'è... deve usare le scale.**	Uh-uh, there isn't one... you have to use the stairs.
SIG. ROSSI:	(to himself) **Che merda! Non c'è un cazzo di ascensore?**	What the fuck! There's no damn elevator?

Use It or Lose It!

The Hotel V quality department is keeping tabs on Elisa to assess her service. Help them fill in the blanks in this phone call made from a *cellulare* with poor reception.

ELISA: Buona sera, Hotel V.

FRANCESCO: Salve, c'è una connessione internet senza fili in ________ (room)?

ELISA: Si, _______ (everywhere in the hotel). ________ (There are) anche videogiochi e video ________ (free).

FRANCESCO: Che altre ___________ (things) ci sono?

ELISA: Molte, c'è un __________ (bar), un _______________ (seafood restaurant), un __________ (spa), una _____________ (pool), una sala riunioni, un servizio di parcheggio per gli __________ (guests), noleggio di __________ (bike) e cellulari, e molte altre piccole cose.

FRANCESCO: Grande, che __________ (hotel) __________ (cool)!

camera; in tutto l'hotel; Ci sono; gratis; cose; bar; ristorante con specialità di pesce; centro benessere; piscina; ospiti; biciclette; hotel; figo

All That Slang

Travel light, travel right... But when it comes to naming your luggage in Italian the same concept of less is more does not apply.

i bagagli	luggage
i bagagli a mano	carry-on luggage
la borsa	bag, purse
la valigia	suitcase
lo zaino	backpack

Use It or Lose It!

Everybody has some luggage, but what is it called? Write the kind of luggage each traveler has.

1. Mario *si è laureato* and decided to thumb it across Italy.
2. Lidia is staying in Milan overnight, on a *viaggio d'affari*, and hasn't the time to wait at the baggage claim.
3. For the summer, Simona is staying with her aunt and uncle at their Tuscan *agriturismo* resort.
4. Daniel is a bum, hitchhiking across southern Italy.

1. lo zaino; 2. i bagagli a mano; 3. la valigia; 4. la borsa

Cara Chiara,

Instead of staying in a typical, boring hotel, I want to try something different on my next trip to Italy. What do you suggest?

Saluti,
Speciale

Caro Speciale:

Apart from hostels, *lo scambio di case*, houseswapping, is becoming more popular by the minute. Just do an online search to find an organization that'll put you in touch with other houseswappers. You pay a small fee, which insures the home against damage, and you may need to sign a contract. Houseswapping is a great way to savor the local culture, and save some money on a long trip. Be sure to ask for plenty of pictures of the place and research the area and organization you select to work with.

Saluti,
Chiara

Quiz Can you pass as a local?

When you travel you...

1. a. speak English to everybody—somebody is bound to understand you.
b. learn some phrases in the country's language—especially the naughty ones!
c. learn the language and memorize your Hide This Book Xtreme.

2. a. arrive with 20 *valigie* and then some. You never know what you are going to need.
b. travel with three *valigie*, enough to last you a week and a half.
c. travel with *bagagli leggeri* (light). You'll get what you need along the way.

3. a. ask if you can use *dollari*.
b. exchange money at the airport and keep it in your pants.
c. exchange a bit of cash at the airport and keep your credit card handy.

4. a. stay at a hotel with a name in English—it's the only brand you trust.
b. stay at a *hotel boutique* with the top amenities in case you hate the city.
c. stay with friends, family or in a hostel—you like to experience the city the way locals do.

5. a. take your most comfortable shoes, shorts and T-shirts; it's your vacation and you plan to dress like it.
b. pack your most stylish clothing. You want to look hot no matter what!
c. know what the locals are wearing before you go. You don't want to stand out!

6. a. find the fast-food joints—you'll survive on burgers and fries.
b. study the travel guides. They've gotta have the best advice, right?
c. ask some locals you meet at a bar, your taxi driver and the clerk at your hotel for recommendations.

7. a. are constantly asked where you're from, even before you open your mouth.
b. are asked where you're from after people talk to you.
c. are asked directions by other *turisti*.

Mostly As

You are the tourist of all tourists, and you're not embarrassed by it. That's OK—it helps you enjoy the city comfortably. Be careful, though: you might be taken advantage of if you're not alert.

Mostly Bs

You try to blend in, but you won't fool anybody. Still, you get a true taste of your vacationing place, and locals appreciate when you make an effort.

Mostly Cs

You can easily pass as a local, though you probably have your I'm-a-tourist-please-help-me moments.

All That Slang

Che tempo fa? So, what's the weather like while you're on your travels?

Che tempo farà?	What will the weather be like?
Pioverà/Nevicherà/Tuonerà/Farà caldo.	It will rain/snow/thunder/be hot.
È la giornata giusta per… una scopatina.	It's a good day for having… a little sex. *Usually used when it's rainy.*
È una giornata perfetta.	The day is perfect.
Piove a catinelle.	It's raining cats and dogs. *Literally, it's raining buckets.*
Fa un caldo assurdo.	It's unbelievably hot.
Che cazzo di freddo!	It's fuckin' cold!
Che cazzo di caldo!	It's fuckin' hot!

Know-it-all/il Saputello

Cielo a pecorelle acqua a catinelle *literally means (more or less) with flocks of sheep in the sky (i.e., small, fluffy clouds), it will rain. Cute, huh?!*

Use It or Lose It!

Pair the pics with a caption from the word bank.

Fa un caldo assurdo.	**Cielo a pecorelle.**
Piove a catinelle.	**Che cazzo di freddo.**

1. It's raining cats and dogs.

2. It's unbelievably hot.

3. It's fuckin' cold.

4. A cloud-dotted sky

1. Piove a catinelle; 2. Fa un caldo assurdo; 3. Che cazzo di freddo; 4. Cielo a pecorelle.

All That Slang

Now that you can talk about the local weather, learn how to talk about the local food.

Ho voglia di arancini.	I'm in the mood for rice balls. *__Arancini__ are stuffed with various ingredients: meat sauce, mozzarella cheese or vegetables.*
Andiamo in un ristorante alla moda.	Let's go to an *in* restaurant. *You could also say __un ristorante in__.*
Che schifo! È troppo grasso.	Disgusting! That's too greasy.
Bleah, fa schifo!	Yuck, that's disgusting!
Mmm, è buonissimo!	Mmm, that's delicious!
Ne vuoi ancora?	Do you want seconds?
No grazie, sono a dieta.	No thanks, I'm on a diet.
Mangia, sei troppo magro♂/magra♀.	Eat, you're too skinny.
Perché non mangi un po' di verdure ogni tanto?	Why don't you eat some vegetables every so often?
Buon appetito!	Enjoy your meal!
Uff! Sto per esplodere.	Oof! I'm about to explode.
Sono pieno♂/piena♀!	I'm so full!
Sto morendo di fame!	I'm dying of hunger!
Spero che ti vada di traverso.	I hope you choke on it.

Use It or Lose It!

What do you say when:

1. ...something is disgusting?
2. ...something is good?
3. ...you want your enemy to choke on it?
4. ...you want someone to enjoy a meal?
5. ...you don't want any more food because you're trying to lose weight?

1. Che schifo.; 2. Mmm, è buonissimo.; 3. Spero che ti vada di traverso.; 4. Buon appetito.; 5. No grazie, sono a dieta.

Food you've gotta try…

1. **pizzoccheri** from Lombardy—whole-grain pasta with savoy cabbage soaked in cheese sauce
2. **nduja** from Calabria—a very spicy, spreadable, seasoned pork meat
3. anything made with **pomodori** (tomatoes)
4. real **polenta**, with stewed meat and vegetables
5. **olive ascolane**—fried, stuffed green olives
6. **mozzarella in carrozza**—fried mozzarella cheese flavored with Parma ham or anchovies
7. **risotto alla milanese**—saffron rice
8. **sugolo**—a wine pudding, made from grapes left over after winemaking; you'll find this jelly-like dessert most often during the winemaking season
9. **salama da sugo**—typical Ferrara sausage mixed with red wine and spices
10. **impepata di cozze**—peppery mussel soup
11. **orecchiette alle cime di rapa**—from Puglia, ear-shaped pasta with turnip tops
12. **tiramisù**—coffee-dipped cake layered with mascarpone cream; literally, **tiramisù** means "cheer me up" *(Note:* ***Tiramisù*** *is also slang for blowjob.)*
13. **cannolo**—from Sicily, an amazing, delightful tube-shaped shell of fried pastry dough filled with ricotta cheese, pistachio bits and candied fruit.
14. **zuppa inglese**—literally, English soup; wedges of sponge cake dipped in liqueur, then covered in thick vanilla and chocolate custard
15. **panna cotta**—a pudding made with cream, milk, sugar and gelatin

Drinks you can't miss…

1. **varnelli**—anise-based liqueur from Marche, typically enjoyed as an **ammazzacaffè**, "coffee-killer", to dull the effects of caffeine
2. **caffè Borghetti**—thick, sweet coffee-flavored liqueur
3. **rum e pera**—separate shots of rum (pronounced **room** in Italian) and pear juice; rum goes down first
4. **limoncello**—a strong lemon-based liqueur from Campania
5. **chinotto**—a non-alcoholic soda with a bitter citrus taste
6. **spritz**—from northern Italy, a light cocktail made with Campari or Aperol and sparkling white wine
7. **bellini**—a glamorous cocktail made of sparkling wine (prosecco or champagne) and peach puree, invented in 1934 by Giuseppe Cipriani, a Venetian bartender
8. **latte e menta**—a refreshing drink with milk and a bit of mint syrup
9. **grappa**—strong liqueur made from fermented peels, seeds and grape stems

All That Slang

Get your groove on by talking about *club, locali e discoteche.*

Quella è una bella discoteca.	That club is good.
Mettono su musica di diversi generi: tecno/pop/rock/reggae.	They play different types of music: techno/pop/rock/reggae.
C'è un gruppo/concerto stasera.	There's a band/an event tonight.
DJ Mingo suona stasera.	DJ Mingo is playing tonight.
Il cocktail di stasera è il bellini.	Tonight's drink is the bellini.
Questa sera...	Tonight...
...due birre al prezzo di una.	...beer is 2 for 1.
...è serata donne. Le ragazze entrano gratis.	...is ladies' night. Girls get in free.
...c'è una partita di calcio.	...there's a soccer game.
...c'è un concerto rock.	...there's a rock concert.
Il biglietto d'ingresso è di 10 €.	The cover is 10 euro.
Non mi piace l'atmosfera.	I don't like the atmosphere.
La discoteca chiude alle 2 di notte.	The club closes at 2 a.m.
È questo l'ingresso per la zona VIP?	Is this the VIP entrance?

VIP in Italian is pronounced vihp.

Use It or Lose It!

Are you cool enough to know where each event happens?

a.

b.

c.

1. **Questa sera c'è una partita di calcio.**
2. **Questa sera c'è un concerto rock.**
3. **Questa sera è serata donne.**

1. c; 2. a; 3. b

 Nice and naughty club speak…

Vuoi ballare?
Do you want to dance?

Ti offro da bere.
I'll buy you a drink.

È la discoteca del momento.
It's the *in* club.

La discoteca è piena di rizzacazzi. 💣💣
The club is full of teases. ***Rizzacazzi*** *are literally dick-lifters.*

Che posto di merda. 💣
What a shitty place.

Cazzo, 'sto posto è stupendo. 💣
This place is fucking awesome.

Cara Chiara:
How can I find a cool Italian club?

Gino

Caro Gino,

Italy is full of party venues and drinking spots. Use common sense when trying to find the best one. Try asking young locals: *Qual è il locale migliore?* Which is the best club? or *Il club più figo?* Is this the coolest club? Hot spots change quickly—what's in today is not in tomorrow, but these additional guidelines will help you:

Check out the crowd—is the place full?

How's the music?

Do they have any good promotions like a special drink or ladies' night?

Who's playing?

Check the décor—if it's too tacky, run.

Sports bars tend to be good on *calcio* (soccer) nights or special events. Otherwise you'll get stuck hanging out with old dudes who don't have cable.

If the cover is too expensive, you can be sure it's either very, very exclusive or it's tourist oriented. It might be good, but you won't get the local flavor.

Saluti,
Chiara

Cara Chiara,
How old do I have to be to get into a bar in Italy?

Giorgio

Caro Giorgio,
Officially, in most Italian places, you have to be 18. Some spots follow a don't ask, don't tell policy, so if you look older, you could get in. Don't embarrass yourself, though, by trying to get in when you're underage.

Saluti,
Chiara

Know-it-all/il Saputello

*In Italy, a **club** (pronounced as in English) is generally an exclusive place or group requiring membership, and not necessarily for dancing. **Discoteca** is a dance club, while **disco-bar** is a pre-clubbing place to start off the night. A **bar** is more often the place you get coffee in the morning, so don't think your Italian friends are alcoholics if they go to the **bar** first thing! A **night** is an adult-only place, like a strip club for example. Don't get 'em mixed up—you might have a more exciting night than you planned!*

All That Slang

If you're gonna be partying, you're gonna need some cash! *Soldi* is the official translation for money, but just like you would say someone has a lot of dough, Italian also has slang terms for *soldi*. Here are a few.

grana — cash
*This can sometimes mean stolen money. Watch out: **Avere delle grane** means to get into a fix, **piantare grane** means to raise a fuss.*

pilla (Genoa) — money

spicci, spiccioli — change, loose change

moneta — coin, money
*__Una moneta__ means one coin, but **la moneta** means the money.*

euri — euro
*Note that **euri** is slang, and isn't the proper term.*

lira — old Italian currency
*It's still used to mean money in general, especially in the phrase **senza una lira** meaning broke.*

denaro — money
A more formal word for money...

Use It or Lose It!

Guess what these people mean as they talk about money.

a. The shop assistant asks you if you want *spicci*.

b. Your ask your Italian friend if you could borrow a few bucks. He tells you that *non ha una lira*.

c. In a movie about a robbery, the main character asks where is the *grana*.

d. A bum begs you to give him *una moneta*.

a. change, loose change; b. he's broke; c. the cash; d. a coin

Dialogue: Non ho una lira.

Carlo and Carlotta are in a restaurant; they just had dinner. When *il conto* comes, Carlo checks his wallet…

CARLO:	**Carlotta, sono al verde.**	Carlotta, I'm broke.
CARLOTTA:	**E io che ci posso fare? Non ho la mia borsa.** (annoyed)	And what am I gonna do about it? I don't have my purse.
CARLO:	**Non so…**	I don't know…
CARLOTTA:	**Sei sicuro di non avere niente?**	Are you sure you don't have anything?
CARLO:	**Non ho una lira.**	Not a cent.
CARLOTTA:	**Sei un pezzente.**	You're a bum.
CARLO:	**Che casino! Ci toccherà lavare i piatti.**	What a mess! We're going to have to do the dishes.
CARLOTTA:	**I piatti! I piatti li pulirà tua nonna. Ciao.**	The dishes! Your grandma can do the dishes. See ya.
CARLO:	**Ma… Carlotta… Aspetta… Carlotta!**	But… Carlotta… Wait… Carlotta!

Word Bytes

essere al verde	to be broke
pezzente	bum
piatti	dishes
pulire	to clean
toccare	to have to

All That Slang

Broke? It's OK to admit it…

Sono a secco.	I'm dried out.
In contanti.	In cash. *Meaning in bank notes, as opposed to checks or other types of payment.*
Devo prelevare.	I need to withdraw.
È povero♂/povera♀.	He/She is poor.

But if you have money…

Sei pieno♂/piena♀ di soldi.	You're loaded.
Sei bombato♂/bombata♀ di soldi.	You're full of money.
È ricco♂/ricca♀.	He/She is rich.
Il portafogli è pieno.	The wallet is fat.

Know-it-all/il Saputello

Wanna go Dutch? In Italian, that's ***pagare alla romana****, literally, to split the bill Roman-style. This means that the whole bill will be split in equal parts—sometimes you lose a bit doing so, but in Italy it's common to be generous with food and drinks, and Italians will often pay for a round or more. So, in the end, you're likely to get more than what you paid for.*

Quiz Loaded or Empty?

Can you accurately say if there is a lot or little cash flow?

1. You know that *sei al verde* when:
a. your wallet is full.
b. your wallet is empty.

2. You know you've got some cash when:
a. *il portafoglio è pieno/gonfio.*
b. *non hai una lira.*

3. You're *ricco*♂/*ricca*♀ when friends say:
a. *sei un*♂/*una*♀ *pezzente.*
b. *sei pieno*♂/*piena*♀ *di soldi.*

4. You gotta file for bankruptcy when:
a. *sei ricco*♂/*ricca*♀.
b. *sei al verde.*

1. b; 2. a; 3. b; 4. b

A-List

Now that you have the cash, get some souvenirs to remember your *viaggio.* Avoid buying plastic magnets; here's a list of must-have souvenirs.

1. Venezia—a *murrina*, a pattern or picture made of long rods of colored glass; an image is revealed when the glass is cut in cross-sections
2. Capri—*sandali capresi*, beautiful handmade leather sandals
3. Firenze—*gioielli in oro* (gold jewelry) sold on the Ponte Vecchio
4. Torino—*gianduiotti*, a chocolate whose shape is similar to an upside-down boat
5. local music you can find only on your travels (no, you can't get it on iTunes®, so don't even bother!)

Know-it-all/il Saputello

If you ever went to Italy—especially in the south of the country—and found yourself all alone in town in the middle of the day, you weren't in the twilight zone! Italians enjoy a midday nap (usually from 1–2 pm), and most stores close at that time and reopen later. Keep in mind that, in Italy, stores open at 10 am and close between 7 and 8 pm. And be sure not to leave your shopping for Sunday—most Italians believe in resting on that day.

All That Slang

Some useful phrases when you are *fare compere* (or *fare shopping*) and trying to get a good deal.

Quanto cosa? How much does it cost?

Ci sono sconti? Are there sales?

In Italy, sales are only at specific times of the year, generally twice a year. Nevertheless, you can often find ***sconti*** *instead, discounts offered by individual shops.*

Mi hanno svenato. They ripped me off.

Le do 10 € e siamo a posto. I'll give you 10 euro and we're good.

Se me lo dà per 5 € lo prendo subito. If you give it to me for 5 euro, I'll take it right now.

1 €, è la mia ultima offerta. 1 euro is my last offer.

Se lo tenga, non mi importa. Keep it, I don't really care.

Quanto mi fa di sconto se ne prendo due? How much less if I buy two?

Use It or Lose It!

Are you ready to bargain in *in italiano*? Match the Italian with the English equivalent.

1. **Mi hanno svenato.**
2. **1 €, è la mia ultima offerta.**
3. **Le do 10 € e siamo a posto.**
4. **Se lo tenga, non mi importa.**
5. **Se me lo dà per 5 € lo prendo subito.**

a. I'll give you 10 euro and we're good.
b. They ripped me off.
c. If you give it to me for 5 euro, I'll take it right now.
d. 1 euro is my last offer.
e. Keep it, I don't really care.

1.b; 2.d; 3.a; 4.e; 5.c

All That Slang

Dove posso comprare...? Where can I buy...? Don't know where to get the essentials

il calzolaio	shoe repair
il ferramenta	hardware store
la gioielleria	jewelry store
la libreria	bookstore
il negozio d'abbigliamento da donna	women's clothing store
il negozio d'abbigliamento da uomo	men's clothing store

Use It or Lose It!

Welcome to *Xtreme Centro Commerciale*, the mall! On your last day of vacation you still have some *compere* (shopping) to do. With the list in hand, find the stores you need and write the name of the store next to the item. The first letter of the name of each store where you found the items will spell a secret word.

Lista dello shopping

- *CD*
- *gioielli in oro*
- *analgesici (painkillers)*
- *vestito*
- *souvenir (tazza, ventaglio)*
- *quadro*
- *slip sexy*

Where to buy: CD, VIP Dischi: gioielli in oro, Aureo Pensiero; analgesici, Cure per Tutti; vestito, Ambi; souvenir (tazza, ventaglio), Nel Paradiso del Turista; quadro, Zoo degli Artisti; slip sexy, Eccitanti Segreti. So what was your secret word? Vacanze, of course!

ere's a short guide.

il negozio d'abbigliamento	clothing store
il negozio di biancheria intima	lingerie store
il negozio di dischi	music store
il negozio di elettronica	electronics store
il negozio di scarpe	shoe store
il parrucchiere	hair salon

chapter 11

Free Time

Get info on:

- the hottest Italian music
- cinema *in italiano*
- what's on TV
- Italian magazines and newspapers

Musica cool

RICCARDO:	**Ehi Giulia, che stai facendo?**	Hey Giulia, what are you doing?
GIULIA:	**Ascolto un po' di musica.**	Just listening to a little music.
RICCARDO:	**Che stai ascoltando?**	What are you listening to?
GIULIA:	**Dell'hip-hop, è il mio genere preferito.**	Hip-hop, it's my favorite kind.
RICCARDO:	**Piace anche a me, però preferisco il rock.**	I like it too, but I like rock better.
GIULIA:	**C'è un concerto di Marracash stasera, andiamoci!**	There's a Marracash concert tonight, let's go!
RICCARDO:	**Va bene, però non lo conosco.**	OK, but I don't know him.
GIULIA:	**Che te ne frega, la musica è figa e i testi dei suoi pezzi spaccano.**	So what, the music is cool and the song lyrics kick ass.
RICCARDO:	**Può venire mia sorella? Anche a lei piace l'hip-hop.**	Can my sister come? She loves hip-hop too.
GIULIA:	**Certo, lo dico al resto della compagnia e andiamo tutti insieme.**	Sure, I'll invite the rest of the guys and we'll all go together.
RICCARDO:	**Figo. Allora ci vediamo stasera.**	Cool. Then I'll see you tonight.

Use It or Lose It!

Can you pass the polygraph? Write *vero* if it's true and *falso* if it's not.

1. Riccardo's favorite music is hip-hop.
2. Riccardo and Giulia are going to a concert tonight.
3. A *compagnia* is a group of friends.
4. Marracash's lyrics are great.
5. Marracash is a hip-hop singer.

1. falso, Riccardo prefers rock; 2. vero; 3. vero; 4. vero; 5. vero

Cara Chiara,

What music do Italian hipsters generally listen to?

Ciao,
Mike

Caro Mike,

In Italy, foreign music has always been very popular. From heavy metal to rap, and from jazz to techno, Italians are very familiar with international artists. There are also many Italian musicians and bands that are just as popular. Lately, hip-hop seems to be the in thing. If you want Italian-style hip-hop, listen in to *neomelodico*, a kind of romantic street-pop music, which originated in Naples. Pop music is very popular among jetsetters, but it's the British version that's hot.

One great thing to discover is Italy's *cantautori*, songwriters from the 70s. With amazing lyrics and talent, they're still as popular today as they were decades ago.

Ciao,
Chiara

Cara Chiara,

I heard some Italian friends from the south speaking of the *tarantella*. My friends were going out to a dance club and they seemed excited. What is it?

Ciao,
Lisa

Cara Lisa,

The *tarantella*, also known as the *taranta*, is a traditional dance from the south. This famous dance is sensuously wild. Back in the day, the dance was used to cure the bite of a spider that could make one hallucinate. The *tarantella* became popular again after several contemporary Italian artists refashioned it with some modern dance twists.

Ciao,
Chiara

All That Slang

You need more entertainment than just music. Here's the slang on movies.

Questo film è...	That movie is...
...una figata.	...a hit.
...molto divertente.	...very funny.
...molto triste.	...very sad.
...molto romantico.	...so romantic.
...è un successone.	...a blockbuster.
...una schifezza.	...garbage.
È una commedia rosa.	It is a pink movie. *Basically, it's a chick flick.*
Che film lento.	What a slow movie.
Che genere di film è?	What type of movie is it?
È...	It's...
...una commedia.	...a comedy.
...una storia d'amore.	...a romance.
...una tragedia.	...a tragedy.
...un drammatico.	...a drama.
...un thriller.	...a suspense film. *The Italian is pronounced* ***triller.***
...un film dell'orrore.	...a horror film.
...un film d'azione.	...an action film.
...un film di arti marziali.	...a martial arts film.
Muoio dalla voglia di vedere quel film.	I'm dying to see that movie. *No need for a doctor! Just go see it.*
Non posso guardare film senza pop corn e una bibita.	I can't watch movies without popcorn and soda.
Perché non stai zitto♂/zitta♀?	Why don't you shut up? *For that jerk who won't let you enjoy the movie.*

If you want to bring out your inner critic, here are a few things you can say about the flicks.

★	**È una cagata.**	It's shit.
★★	**Così così.**	So, so.
★★★	**Bello.**	Good.
★★★★	**Un successo, una figata.**	A hit, super cool.

Use It or Lose It!

Bea is a first-time critic on a radio show. She's so nervous, she doesn't know what to say. Help her get her words out, in Italian. She thinks that:

1. The movie is a blockbuster but it is slow.

   ____

2. It's a chick flick, and it's funny.

   ____

3. The movie is shit.

   ____

4. There's another movie that she's dying to see.

   ____

1. **È un film di successo però è lento.**; 2. **È una commedia rosa, è divertente.**; 3. **È una cagata.**; 4. **Muoio dalla voglia di vedere quel film.**

Quiz

Are you a movie geek?

1. When you go to the movies you buy:
  a. your *biglietto* (ticket), and nothing else. You don't like being distracted.
  b. *popcorn* and soda to munch while you enjoy the movie.
  c. *popcorn,* soda and chocolates, enough to last you two weeks. You spend the movie eating and throwing your snacks at people.

2. You get your *biglietto:*
  a. at least one hour before the movie starts.
  b. 15 to 30 minutes before it starts, so you get in after the commercials.
  c. as a distraction after an unsuccessful shopping day. It doesn't matter if the movie already started.

3. Your favorite time to go to the movies is:
  a. if it's a great movie, you'll be at the premiere, no matter what time it is.
  b. a weekend night. It's a good way to start a long weekend.
  c. never, you'd rather rent the DVD.

4. You agree with the *critici cinematografici* (film critics):
  a. almost always, in fact, you send them recommendations.
  b. almost never, you loved all three Die Hards!
  c. *Critici?* You don't know and you don't care.

Mostly As

The seats at your nearest *cinema* have an imprint of your butt. You might want to give it a break… or not.

Mostly Bs

You like going to the movies, but you also like doing other things. Good for you.

Mostly Cs

You couldn't care less about the movies! You've got better ways to spend your free time.

Use It or Lose It!

These are the movies showing at the fictional Cinema di Pomaretto Marittima. What type of movies are they: *commedia romantica*, *film d'azione* or *film thriller*?

1. **Il fuoco della vendetta** (The Fire of Vengeance)
   Yoel lost his house and his family in a fire, then he lost his friends when he was blamed for it. After 10 years in jail, he is out with a vengeance, looking for who framed him.
2. **Amori di gioventù** (Young Love)
   Luisa and Anthony were high school sweethearts but life got in the way. Fifteen years later they meet again; they dismiss their love as a thing of the past, but fate thinks otherwise.
3. **Corri, Rosa** (Run, Rosa)
   Rosa borrowed money from the mob. She's behind on her payments, and she must return it before 10 p.m. or the mob will kill her lover.

film d'azione; commedia romantica; film thriller

All That Slang

TV lingo for couch potatoes...

Abbassa/Alza il volume. — Turn down/up the volume.

Danno qualcosa di bello? — Are they showing anything good?

Non c'è niente. — There's nothing on.

A forza di guardare la TV, ti stai rincoglionendo. — Watching TV all day is making you stupid.

Ci sono rimasto♂/rimasta♀ sotto, a questo programma. — I'm addicted to this show.

Mi sono perso♂/persa♀ la puntata di *Lost* di ieri sera. — I missed last night's episode of *Lost*.

Raccontami che è successo. — Tell me what happened.

Aggiornami sulla soap. — Catch me up on the soap.

Watch your Italian pronunciation of soap: ***soh-app****.*

Use It or Lose It!

What would you say if…

1. …you want to know if there will be anything good on TV?
2. …it's 2 a.m. and there are only infomercials on TV?
3. …you want to tell your friend that he's watching too much TV?
4. …you're considering a 12-step plan for your addiction to soap operas?
5. …you're pissed for missing last Saturday's SNL episode?
6. …you need your friend to tell you what happened last week in the soap?
7. …you want your friend to tell you what happened?
8. …your ears are about to explode?

a. **Non c'è niente.**
b. **Abbassa il volume.**
c. **Ci sono rimasto♂/rimasta♀ sotto, a questo programma.**
d. **Danno qualcosa di bello?**
e. **Aggiornami sulla soap.**
f. **Mi sono perso♂/persa♀ la puntata del *SNL* di ieri sera.**
g. **Raccontami che è successo.**
h. **A forza di guardare la TV, ti stai rincoglionendo.**

1.d; 2.a; 3.h; 4.c; 5.f; 6.e; 7.g; 8.b

Don't miss these shows and series.

Boris

www.borisblog.tv

In this Italian parody on soap operas, Boris is one of the characters' lucky goldfish. The series is one of the few 100% Italian productions out there!

Cameracafé

www.cameracafe.it

These short sketches, caught by a camera in an office coffee machine, capture the lives of silly professionals. Funny and fast-paced, this sitcom is great for learning Italian.

Le Iene

www.iene.mediaset.it

Hidden cameras capture the countless real-life political and social scandals of the country, with a touch of irony.

All That Slang

Get cultured, *in italiano. Che vuoi fare?* What would you rather do?

Vedere uno spettacolo teatrale.	Watch a play.
Andare a un concerto.	Go to a concert.
Andare all'opera.	Go to the opera.
Vedere un balletto.	See a ballet.
Vedere uno spettacolo.	Watch a performance.
Andare al circo.	Go to the circus.
Vedere un musical.	Watch a musical.

Everybody's a critic. Talking about performances…

È uno spettacolo sperimentale, non lo capisce nessuno.	It is an experimental performance; nobody understands it.
Mi hanno detto che lo spettacolo teatrale era stupendo/uno schifo.	They told me that the play was excellent/awful.
Il musical era noioso/divertente.	The musical was boring/fun.
Il coro ha cantato divinamente/in modo pessimo.	The choir sang wonderfully/terribly.
Il violinista ♂/La violinista ♀ è eccellente/terribile.	The violinist is excellent/terrible.
Il ballerino ♂/La ballerina ♀ è caduto ♂/caduta ♀.	The dancer fell.
Uff, era troppo lungo.	Ugh, it was too long.

Use It or Lose It!

Can you pass the polygraph? Write *vero* if it's true and *falso* if it's not.

1. If the *ballerina* was good, she was *terribile.*
2. If *l'opera era noiosa*, then it was awesome.
3. You'd rather *andare a un concerto* than *vedere un balletto.*
4. *Il concerto* was good because it was *troppo lungo.*

1. Falso: she was eccellente. Terribile means terrible.
2. Falso: Noioso♂/Noiosa♀ means it was boring.
3. That is really up to you.
4. Falso: if the concert was good you wouldn't think it was troppo lungo: too long.

Cool lit...

il topo di biblioteca
Mmm...
Mi piace leggere di tutto: libri, riviste, quotidiani, classici, vignette...
I like reading everything: books, magazines, newspapers, classics, comic strips...
l'intellettuale
Secondo Platone...
According to Plato...
l'equilibrata
La Divina Commedia
il fannullone
per domani
for tomorrow

Word Bytes

i classici	classics
equilibrato♂/equilibrata♀	well-rounded
il fannullone♂/ la fannullona♀	slacker *Another popular word is* ***perditempo****.*
il giornale, il quotidiano	newspaper
l'intellettuale	intellectual
il libro	book
la rivista	magazine
il topo di biblioteca	bookworm *literally, library mouse*
le vignette, i fumetti	comic strips

Quiz What type of reader are you?

1. *Leggi* (you read):
   - **a.** *tutti i giorni* (every day) for fun.
   - **b.** *tutti i giorni* so that you can keep up in class discussions.
   - **c.** *mai* (never).
   - **d.** *una o due volte alla settimana* (once or twice a week).
2. Your favorite genre is:
   - **a.** *tutti* (everything).
   - **b.** history, philosophy and *classici*.
   - **c.** *le vignette* (but only if you're forced to read something).
   - **d.** *riviste e bestseller.*
3. In a conversation about *libri*, you:
   - **a.** don't really talk. That would mean you'd have to put your book down!
   - **b.** dominate the conversation. You lose control when talking about books.
   - **c.** are completely bored out of your mind.
   - **d.** can keep up, if you feel like it.
4. The last thing you read was:
   - **a.** Umberto Eco's *Il Nome della Rosa* (The Name of the Rose), some news articles, your Italian textbook…
   - **b.** All the top books from the New York Times book review.
   - **c.** *La Divina Commedia*…Cliff Notes.
   - **d.** A *rivista di moda* (fashion magazine), *il giornale* and half a chapter of Giorgio Faletti's latest *romanzo.*

Mostly As
You are a *topo di biblioteca*. You devour books like there is no tomorrow.

Mostly Bs
You are an *intellettuale*. You read a lot, and you like to let people know you do.

Mostly Cs
You are a *fannullone*. You hate reading (or anything that requires energy).

Mostly Ds
You are *equilibrato*♂/*equlibrata*♀, a well-rounded reader.

Cara Chiara:

I'm a total *topo di biblioteca*, but I want the time I spend reading to be productive too. Is reading a good way to learn Italian?

Saluti, Lexy

Cara Lexy:

Sure, why not?! Look for books with bilingual editions, or read the newspaper, magazines or a blog. If you want a break from books, you can watch TV shows like soap operas (*or telenovele*) or movies with subtitles in Italian—that way you can listen and read.

Saluti, Chiara

Bad Language

Get info on:

- cursing
- how to know you've been insulted
- how to fight back

DISCLAIMER 

We don't recommend using these words and expressions but in case you overhear them, we want you to know what people are saying! We are not responsible if you get a black eye or a rearranged smile from using these insults. Warning! There are no 💣💣 in this chapter, because all the language is bad!

A-List: Top 10 *parolacce*

cazzo — fuck *Literally, this means something like cock, but it's a much more versatile curse word.*

merda — shit

stronzo — asshole, dumb ass *literally, turd*

a tua madre — your momma *Literally, to your mother, this phrase is a cruel reply to any insult.*

figlio ♂ / figlia ♀ di puttana — son of a bitch *In Italian, you can say son or daughter of a bitch.*

non rompermi… — don't break… *Use this and you'd be telling someone, in a nasty way, that you don't want to be bothered, e.g.,* ***non rompermi il cazzo, non rompermi i coglioni****, etc.*

fottere — to fuck/screw ***Me ne fotto*** *means I don't give a fuck.*

stocazzo, sticazzi — no fucking way *You'll also hear* ***stica****, shorthand.*

i coglioni — balls *Wanna be a tad less vulgar? Use* ***le palle*** *instead. In other situations, it implies courage:* ***quello ha le palle/i coglioni*** *(he's got balls).*

bastardo — bastard *It may be mild in English, but in Italian, it's harsh.*

Use It or Lose It!

Meet Joe W. He is the biggest asshole you'll ever meet. Look at the things people have said about him, and see if you can describe him in English. Write the translation next to the Italian.

MEET JOE W.

1. He's a **figlio di puttana**.
2. His favorite curse word is **cazzo**.
3. He is a **stronzo**.
4. He has **le palle**.
5. He is full of **merda**.

1. a son of a bitch
2. fuck
3. asshole
4. balls
5. shit

Know-it-all/il Saputello

If you were to learn only one Italian curse word, **cazzo** *should be the one. It's similar to fuck, but it's much more than that. It's one of the most versatile and confusing terms in the Italian language, and it's also used throughout Italy.*

Said in anger, **cazzo** *is a strong insult:* **Cazzo di uomo! Cazzo dici? Cazzo fai?** *What a fucking loser! What the fuck are you saying? What the fuck are you doing? Here are a few more variants:*

Cazzone *is like saying "you stupid ass" in an affectionate way, as well as saying someone is a bit of a loser.*

Una cazzata *is a fuck-up or a stupid thing.*

Sono incazzato ♂ **/incazzata** ♀ *= I'm pissed off.*

Mi fa incazzare *= That pisses me off.*

What the fuck can be simply **che cazzo**.

The word is so common that it's also used as a filler, like "like" or "um" in English.

Use It or Lose It!

Fill in the correct usage of *cazzo* for each picture.

a. **Che cazzo!** b. **Ciao, cazzone!** c. **Cazzo fai?** d. **Che cazzata!**

1.c; 2.a; 3.d; 4.b

Dear Chiara,

My Italian friends are guttermouths, and I want to keep up. What nasty words should I know?

Yours,
Patty Mouz

Cara Patty:

These are the *parolacce* that did not make the countdown...

figa
It is used just like *cazzo*, especially in Milan.

belìn
In Genoa, this equals *cazzo*.

sborone
Common in Emilia-Romagna, it refers to a person who thinks he/she is better than the rest. Use *presuntuoso* outside this region.

puttana, troia
Basically these mean bitch or whore. While a *puttana* refers more to the job, a *troia* is more of a slut, or a cheater.

porca troia
Literally it means dirty slut, but is used like "what the fuck".

leccaculo
This is a person who kisses ass to climb the ladder.

quaquaraqua
This is an expression that's been around for a long time, and is still in use today. It defines a person with no guts, a coward.

Vai a fare in culo!/Vaffanculo!/Fanculo!
Three ways to say fuck off.

Use It or Lose It!

What did that potty mouth just say? Complete the naughty expressions.

a. **Sei uno** ______________________________.

b. **A tua** ______________________________.

c. **Tu mi fai** ______________________________.

d. **Sei un idiota; sei un** ______________________________.

e. ______________________________**! Che male!**
______________________________**!**

a. stronzo; b. madre; c. incazzare; d. coglione; e. Cazzo; Merda

Le ragazze per bene possono dire le parolacce?

Can polite ladies curse?

Cazzo! Merda! Figa! Porca troia!
Fuck! Shit! Fuck! What the fuck!
Ahi!
Ouch!

Use It or Lose It!

Can you remember what these words mean?

a. **Cazzo!**
b. **Merda!**
c. **Figa!**
d. **Porca troia!**

a. Fuck! Used in anger or pain.; b. The equivalent of shit.; c. Milan's slang for cazzo.; d. What the fuck!

Gentle ways to express anger and the not-so-gentle…

Cavolo!
Drat!

Literally, Cabbage! The switcharoo of ***cazzo*** *with* ***cavolo*** *makes this senseless phrase work.*

Vai a quel paese.
Eff off.

Literally, Go to that country. If ***vaffanculo*** *(fuck off) is literally* ***vai a fare in culo*** *(something like go to the ass), then the above expression is a more polite way to suggest another destination.*

Figlio di buona donna!
Son of a gun!

Literally, Son of a good woman! This is the opposite of ***figlio di puttana****, son of a bitch, but the meaning is the same.*

Porca miseria!
What the heck!

Literally, Damn misery! This phrase is a gentler way to express ***porca troia****.*

Pezzo di merda.
Piece of shit.

Nasty!

Levati dal cazzo.
Get the fuck out of here.

Your message will be understood loud and clear.

Che due coglioni!
What balls!

Succhiacazzi!
Cocksucker!

È rimasto di merda.
He was left like a piece of shit.

Used when someone is left speechless or is overcome by embarrassment or guilt.

Use It or Lose It!

Write the PG substitute for each curse word.

1. **Cazzo.**
2. **Porca troia.**
3. **Figlio di puttana!**
4. **Vaffanculo!**

1. Cavolo.; 2. Porca miseria.; 3. Figlio di buona donna!; 4. Vai a quel paese!

Quiz How dirty are you?

For each situation, choose one way of responding. You will get points depending on how you respond—the dirtier, the better.

1. Your just received your paper on how to make the world *verde*. You got a crappy score with a frowning face (your teacher has a childish sense of humor). Meanwhile, your best friends are very excited because they all got high marks (and a smiley), and one of them comes over to tell you. You say:
a. *Cavolo.*
b. *Cazzo.*

2. Someone just cut you off while you were driving. He gives you the finger, and you almost hit another car. You scream:
a. *Porca miseria!*
b. *Porca troia!*

3. You've been dying for a double hot fudge brownie sundae with extra cherries. When you finally get it, the *nerd* kid working the counter trips and throws it on your white T-shirt. You shout:
a. *Vaffanculo.*
b. *Vai a quel paese.*

4. You are getting so bored by the movie your friend recommended. You think to yourself:
a. *Mi sono rotto i coglioni!*
b. *Mi sono rotto i maroni!*

5. Your best friend is mocking you.
a. *Figlio di buona donna!*
b. *Figlio di puttana!*

1. a=1 point, b=2 points; 2. a=1 point, b=3 points; 3. a=5 points, b=2 points; 4. a=3 points, b=1 point; 5. a=2 points, b=3 points

If you had 10 or more points you are just mean! Congratulations, you have a very good extended vocabulary.

If you had 9 points or fewer you are a bit of a goody two-shoes. Work on your dark side; you never know when you might need it.

All That Slang

A course in curse… Learn the proper ways to be improper.

Porca puttana vacca troia!	What the fucking fuck! *Literally, Damn dirty whore bitch!*
Cazzo di stronzo.	What a load of a shit. *You can substitute* **stronzo** *with anything and anyone.*
Cazzo credi, che stia qui a farmi le seghe?	What do you think I was doing, jacking off? *Use this when someone accuses you of procrastinating.*
Che stronzata!	Bullshit!
Me ne fotto!	I don't give a fuck!
Fottitinne!	Just give a fuck! *A suggestion not to over worry; used in Campania.*
Shfacimm'.	What a mess. *A mess, just harsher…*
Quello lì si fa troppe pugnette.	That guy worries too much. *Literally, That guy jacks off too much. Said in Emilia-Romagna.*
Me cojoni!	What balls! *A trademark of Rome.*
Va'mmorì ammazzato.	I wish you'd die. *It's a very common expression in Rome, also used between friends. Watch out if you use it though, it can be very harsh.*
Segaiolo.	Wanker. *Tuscans love this one.*
Bottana.	Whore. *A favorite of Sicily.*
Figghi 'n drocchia.	Son of a bitch. *You'll hear this in Calabria.*
A mammeta, a sorta, a frateta.	(Screw) Your mother, your sister, your brother.
Mona.	Jerk. *It can be mellow or harsh, depending on the context. You'll hear it in Veneto.*
Cugghione!	Asshole! *Used in Puglia.*
N'culo a mammeta/a soreta.	Go fuck your mother's/sister's ass. *Said in southern Italy.*
Va' dà via el cu.	Go get fucked in the ass. *Courtesy of Lombardy.*

Use It or Lose It!

Carlo received this *e-mail* from his friend Pietro, but he left out all the curses! Can you help him turn this into an R-rated e-mail?

Hey __________ (dude)

_______________! (Fuck) The soccer game was ________ (shit). __________ (It pisses me off) that we lost. __________! (Fuck) Laura didn't come 'cause she had a zit. I told her __________ (fuck off) and she got pissed off at me. Whatever, __________ (I don't give a fuck).

See you later, __________ (dude)

Pietro

cazzone; Cazzo; una merda; Mi fa incazzare; Cazzo; vaffanculo;
me ne fotto; cazzone

Dialogue: The interview

Federica is a news reporter for the network Rete 4. Her first assignment is to interview Filippo, the Italian heartthrob. Unfortunately, he is in a bad mood…

FEDERICA:	**Filippo, si dice che hai una nuova amante.**	Filippo, rumor is that you have a new lover.
FILIPPO:	**Che cazzo te ne frega?**	Why the fuck do you care?
FEDERICA:	**Quindi, non è vero?** (confused)	Then, it's not true?
FILIPPO:	**Ma perchè non vi fate tutti un po' i cazzi vostri?**	Why don't you care a little more about your own fucking business?
FEDERICA:	**Ma, Filippo, non mi sembra il caso.**	But, Filippo, it's not a big deal.
FILIPPO:	**Ma sticazzi che non ti sembra il caso? Mi hanno rotto i coglioni sempre con la stessa domanda del cazzo.**	So it's not a fucking big deal? I'm tired of being asked the same fucking question.
FEDERICA:	**Beh, scusa, cambiamo argomento.**	Well sorry, let's change the subject.
FILIPPO:	**Ottima idea.**	Excellent idea.

FEDERICA: **Vuoi dire qualcosa ai tuoi fan?**	Do you want to send a message to your fans?
FILIPPO: **Sì, che li amo, anche se sono delle merde. Ciao!**	Yes, that I love them, even though they're all shit. Ciao!
FEDERICA: **Sei uno sboccato.**	You're a potty mouth.

Word Bytes

Sticazzi che…?	So it's not a fucking...? *Just repeat what's been told to you adding* ***sticazzi che*** *to mean someone is talking bullshit.*
i cazzi miei/tuoi/suoi/nostri/vostri/loro	my/your/his/her/our/your/their fucking business
Che cazzo te ne frega?	Why the fuck do you care?
Sei uno sboccato♂/una sboccata♀.	You're a potty mouth.

Use It or Lose It!

Frederica's interview was censored by Rete 4. Exchange the *bips* with Filippo's curses.

FEDERICA: **Filippo, si dice che hai una nuova amante.**

FILIPPO: **Che -bip- te ne frega.**

FEDERICA: **Quindi, non è vero?**

FILIPPO: **Ma perchè non vi fate tutti un po' i -bip- vostri?**

FEDERICA: **Ma Filippo, non mi sembra il caso.**

FILIPPO: **Ma -bib- che non ti sembra il caso? Mi hanno rotto i -bip- sempre con la stessa domanda del -bip- .**

FEDERICA: **Beh, scusa, cambiamo argomento.**

FILIPPO: **Ottima idea.**

FEDERICA: **Vuoi dire qualcosa ai tuoi fan?**

FILIPPO: **Sì, che li amo, anche se sono delle -bip-. Ciao!**

cazzo, cazzi, sticazzi, coglioni, cazzo, merde

Use It or Lose It!

Think of this as the R-rated version of the Sunday crossword puzzle.

Across

3 someone performing a vulgar act, solo

4 the most useful word to insult in Italian

5 what a guy from Milan might say instead of *cazzo*

9 a jerk in Veneto

10 soccer has one, a guy has two

11 a turd, behaving like an asshole

13 term for shit

14 Bullshit!

15 a woman working the streets

Down

1 a hypocrite pretending to be nice

2 a fast way to say fuck off

5 offspring of a bad woman

6 a son of a bitch

7 (screw) your mother, in Calabria

8 if you're full of yourself, you are a...

12 a friend or a loser

Across: 3. segaiolo; 4. cazzo; 5. figa; 9. mona; 10. coglione; 11. stronzo; 13. merda 14. chestronzata; 15. puttana Down: 1. leccaculo; 2. vaffanculo; 5. figliodiputtana; 6. bastardo; 7. amammeta; 8. sborone; 12. cazzone

Anti-dictionary

You're not gonna find the typical terms in this dictionary, but you will find all of the cool terms, slanguage and swear words used in this book, and then some. Other things you should note:

- Who says a dictionary has gotta be A to Z? This one is Z to A!
- Don't know if a noun is feminine or masculine? If it says *il* or *lo* it's masculine, and *la* or *l'* it's feminine. There are a few exceptions. Don't worry; we'll let you know!
- Look for ♂/♀ to figure out how to gender-bend adjectives.

zit il brufolo 79

zipper la patta 71

your tuo♂/tua♀ (singular) 31, 33, 36, 40, 44, 47, 82, 98, 113, 116, tuoi♂/tue♀ (plural) 121

you tu (informal) 13, 34, 35, 42, 47, 116, lei (formal)

yellow il giallo 44, 76

yeah right come no 60

W

wrinkle la ruga 77, 78

worry, to preoccuparsi 77

world il mondo 23

work, to funzionare (function, operate) 66

work interview il colloquio di lavoro 72

word scramble il crucipuzzle 62, 82

wooden in legno 75, 76

wonderfully divinamente 110

woman la donna 43, 95, 102

wireless wireless, senza fili 66, 89

wine il vino 17, 87

window la finestra 75, 76

wife la moglie 24

why perché 34, 41, 42, 52, 53, 93, 106, 120, 121

whore la puttana 113, 114, 115, 117, 118, 119, 122, la bottana 💣 (Sicily) 119

who chi 20, 21, 79, 80

white il bianco 45, 76

whiny piagnone♂/piagnona♀ 23

when quando 35, 36, 37, 84, 85

wheel ghiera (iPod®) 65

what che (pronoun) 9, 11, 20, 21, 22, 23, 31, 34, 35, 36, 37, 42, 63, 71, 72, 74, 88, 89, 92, 96, 98, 104, 106, 108, 109, 110, 117, cosa (question or exclamation) 20, 29, 47, 60, 71, 72

well-rounded equilibrato♂/equilibrata♀ 111, 112

well bene 36, 51, beh (filler between words in spoken language) 23, 120, 121

week la settimana 112

Wednesday il mercoledì 36

website il sito 49, il portale 49, il sito web 48, 49, 53, la pagina web 49

weather il tempo 92

wear, to mettersi 71, 72

water l'acqua 45, 81

watch, to guardare 86, 106, 108, 109

watch l'orologio 70

wash, to lavare 35, 45, 98

want, to volere 23, 33, 36, 42, 44, 45, 56, 57, 78, 93, 96, 118, 121

wanker il segaiolo 💣 119, 122

wallet il portafogli 99, 100

wall la parete (inner) 75, il muro (outer) 75

wait, to aspettare 34, 35, 36, 52, 98

V

vomit, to vomitare 79

voicemail la voicemail 66

virginity sverginare (to take someone's virginity) 39, 43, 45

VIP il/la VIP (pronounced *vihp*) 95, 103

violinist il/la violinista 110

vintage la vendemmia (as in wine) 85, 86

view, to visualizzare 56, 64

view vista (landscape) 88

videogame console la console 61, 62

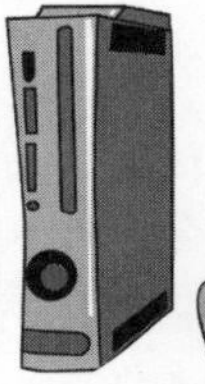

videogame il videogioco 88, 89

video player il lettore video 61

video il video 51, 56, 60, 65, 88, 89

vibrate vibrazione (cellphone) 64

vegetables le verdure 93

vagina la vagina 9

vacation la vacanza 102

U

used usato (worn out, second hand) 81

use, to usare 39, 82, 88

URL l'indirizzo 48

upload, to caricare 56, 57

undress, to spogliarsi 39

underwear la biancheria 70, 103

undershirt la canottiera 70

under sotto 20, 31, 69

un-cool sfigato♂/sfigata♀ 11, 12, 13, schifo (garbage, disgusting) 11, 79, 81, 93, fa pena 11

uncle lo zio 23

ugly brutto♂/brutta♀ 11, 12

T

typical tipico 23

two due 44, 95, 101, 112, 113, 117

twice due volte 112

TV la TV (pronounced *tee-voo*) 65, 108, 109

tuxedo lo smoking 69, 70

turn up, to alzare (as in volume) 108

turn down, to abbassare (as in volume) 108, 109

T-shirt la maglietta 12, 13, la T-shirt 12, 70, 72

true vero♂/vera♀ 21, 63, 75, 105, 110, 120, 121

trip il viaggio 82, 90, 100

tree hugger l'ecologista 81, 82, 83

transvestite il travestito 27, il travello 27, 28, il travone 27, 28

transexual il transessuale 27

tragedy la tragedia 106

trade, to scambiare 74, 75, 90

tourist il/la turista 102, 103

touch, to (oneself) toccarsi 39, 44

top attivo (sexual) 31

too much troppo 8, 35, 36, 37, 71, 73, 82, 93, 110

tonight stasera 31, 32, 35, 47, 49, 95, 104

tongue la lingua 40

tomorrow domani 35, 111

tomato il pomodoro 94

tolerate, to sopportare 23, 41, 42

together, to be stare con 20, 44

together insieme 42, 43, 52, 53, 104

today oggi 10, 55

tits le tette, 38, 44, i meloni 38

times le volte (repetitions) 78, 112

tie la cravatta (accessory) 70, 72

ticket il biglietto 107

thunder, to tuonare 92

thriller il drammatico (genre) 106

threesome una cosa a tre 19

this questo 45, 53, 56, 57, 63, 66, 69, 78, 88, 95, 106, 108, 109, 'sto (short-hand) 11, 96

think, to pensare 10, 74, saltare in mente (to go through someone's head) 71

thermos thermos 82

thanks grazie 12, 81, 88, 93

text, to mandare un messaggio 49, mandare un SMS 49

testicles le palle (balls) 💣 38, 113, 114

terrible tremendo♂/tremenda♀ 79, 80, terribile 79, 80, 110

tense teso♂/tesa♀ 77

tell, to raccontare 108, 109, dire 20, 21, 29, 34, 45, 110, 116

telephone il telefono 66

techno la techno (music) 95

tech support il tecnico 66

tease la rizzacazzi 💣💣 96

taste il gusto 74, 75, 76

tan, to prendere il sole 84

talk, to parlare 37

tacky sdolcinato♂/sdolcinata♀ (in a romantic sense) 41, 42, 43, 44, di cattivo gusto (in bad taste) 74, 75

table il tavolo 75

S

sync, to sincronizzare 66

swimming pool la piscina 45, 75, 76, 88, 89

sweater il pullover 70

suspense il thriller (film genre) 106, 108

surf, to navigare (internet) 49

sure sicuro♂/sicura♀ 20, 44, 49, 98

supermarket il supermercato 83

superb eccellente 110

sunglasses gli occhiali da sole 70, 72

Sunday la domenica 12, 13, 35

suitcase la valigia 89, 90, 91

suit il completo 70

suck, to succhiare (action) 39, fare pena (to be disappointing) 11, sucare 💣💣 (sexual) (southern Italy) 39

subject l'argomento 120, 121

stupid ass il cazzone♂/la cazzona♀ 💣 114, 115, 120, 122

stupid scemo♂/scema♀ 35, idiota 116

stunning stupendo♂/stupenda♀ 7, 8, 36, 37, 74, 96, 110

strip club il night 97

stretch, to fare stretching 77

stress lo stress 77, 78

stove top il fornello 75

story la storia (also means relationship) 20, 22, 106

store il negozio 102, 103

stopwatch il cronometro 65

steaming bollente 43

STD le malattie veneree (MST) 79

start l'inizio 44

stand, to sopportare 23, 41, 42

stallion lo stallone 43

spinster la zitella 15, 16, 23

spectacular meraviglioso♂/meravigliosa♀ 8

specialty la specialità (cuisine) 88, 89

special particolare 34, speciale 90

spasm, to have a (neck) avere il torcicollo 77, 78

sparkling wine prosecco 94

souvenir il souvenir 102

sorry, to be dispiacersi 35

sorry scusa (I am sorry) 7, 10, 13, 66, 120, 121

soon presto 35

song la canzone 66

son of a bitch figlio♂/figlia♀ di puttana 💣💣 113, 114, 117, 118, figlio♂/figlia♀ di buona donna 💣💣 (less rude) 117, 118, figghi' n drocchia 💣💣 (Calabria) 119

son il figlio 15

something qualcosa 108, 109

sofa il divano 75, 76

soda la bibita (non-alcoholic beverage) 106

sock il calzino 37, 69, 70

soccer il calcio 95, 96

soap opera la soap 108, 109, la telenovela 112

soap il sapone 83

so così 51, così così (so-so) 106

snob fighetto♂/fighetta♀ 15, 16, 17, fichetto♂/fichetta♀ 15

snack lo snack 88

smog lo smog 82

slow down, to rallentare 35

slow lento♂/lenta♀ 106, 107

slacker il fannullone♂/la fannullona♀ 111, 112

skirt la gonna 70, 71, 73

skinny magro♂/magra♀ 93

sister la sorella 29, 74, 81, 85, 86, 104

sink il lavello (kitchen) 75, il lavandino (bathroom) 76

sincerely sinceramente 33

silly scemo♂/scema♀ 35

silent silenzioso♂/silenziosa♀ 64

signal la linea (phone) 63, 66

sightseeing il giro turistico 85

shut up, to stare zitto♂/zitta♀ 106

shuffle casuale (music players) 65

show il programma (TV) 65, 108, 109

shoulder la spalla 78

shop, to fare shopping 101

shoe repair store il calzolaio 102

shoe la scarpa 70, 71, 72, 73, 103

shitty di merda 💣 96

shit, to cacare 💣 79, 80

shit la merda 💣 82, 113, 114, 116, 117, 120, 122

share, to condividere 56, 57

sexy sexy 55, 71, 102

sex, to have fare sesso 39

sex il sesso (also meaning gender) 48

settings le impostazioni 64, 65

service il servizio 88, 89

serenade la serenata 41

sentence la frase 37, 44

send, to inviare 48, 64, mandare 47, 48, 50, spedire 48

select, to selezionare 64, 65

see, to vedere 35, 37, 42, 43, 45, 56, 57, 71, 74, 104, 106, 107, 110

search, to cercare 49, 50, 53, 54, 55

seafood il pesce (fish) 88, 89

sea il mare 45, 87, 88

screw, to fottere 💣 82, 113

screen lo schermo 61, 62, 64

scissors la forbice (sex) 39

school la scuola 77, 85, 86

scared spaventato♂/spaventata♀ 19

say, to dire 20, 21, 29, 34, 45, 110, 116

Saturday il sabato 35

sandal il sandalo 100

same uguale 32, stesso♂/stessa♀ 44, 120, 121

sad triste 106

s.o.b. figlio♂/figlia♀ di puttana 💣💣 113, 114, 117, 118, figlio♂/figlia♀ di buona donna (less rude) 117, 118, figghi' n drocchia 💣💣 (Calabria) 119

R

rum il rum 94

rub, to strusciarsi 39

room la stanza 75, la camera 74, 75, 76, 88, 89

romantic romantico♂/romantica♀ 45, 106, 108

romance la storia d'amore 106

rocker il rocchettaro♂/la rocchettara♀ 23

rock il rock (music) 95, 104

rise, to alzarsi (also to get up) 78

ringtone la suoneria 64

right now subito 47, 101

right come no (yeah, right sure) 60, la destra (direction) 40

ridiculous ridicolo♂/ridicola♀ 23, 71, 73

richie figlio♂/figlia♀ di papà 15

rice risotto (in some recipies) 94

reverse indietro 64, 65

reset, to resettare 66

request la richiesta 53

reply, to rispondere 48

repeat, to ripetere 78

rental il noleggio 88, 89

remember, to ricordare 84

relaxed tranquillo♂/tranquilla♀ 37

relax, to rilassarsi 77, 78

reggae il reggae 95

refrigerator il frigorifero, il frigo 75

reduce, to ridurre 82

red il rosso 44, 76

recycle, to riciclare 82

recharge, to ricaricare 66

receive, to ricevere 64

really veramente 47, 71, davvero 36, 37

ready pronto♂/ pronta♀ 35, 37

read, to leggere 55, 56, 111, 112

rain, to piovere 92

Q

quit, to uscire (PC) 49

question la domanda 120, 121

pussy la fica 💣 38, la passera 💣 38, la gnocca 💣 38

purse la borsa 89, 98

purple il viola 45, 76

proud fiero♂/fiera♀ 31, 32

program il programma (PC and TV) 49, 65, 108, 109

profile il profilo 47, 54, 59

printer la stampante 60, 61, 62

print, to stampare 48, 60

princess la principessa 31, 33

price il prezzo 95

potty mouth sboccato♂/sboccata♀ 121

popular novel il bestseller 112

poor povero♂/povera♀ 99

pollution l'inquinamento 82

podcast il podcast 65

playlist la playlist 65

player il lettore (tech) 60, 61, 67

play for the other team, to essere sull'altra sponda 29, 30

play, to suonare (music) 95, play (button) 65

play spettacolo teatrale (drama) 110

pissed off incazzato♂/incazzata♀ 114

pirate il pirata 49

pink il rosa 45, 76, 106, 107

pillow il cuscino 75, 76

pill la pillola 79, l'anticoncezionale (birth control) 80

piece il pezzo 117

pick-up line la frase per abbordare 37, 44

pick up, to (something) prendere (catch) 34, 36

pick-up abbordare (social) 37, 44

photo la foto 53, 54, 63, 65, 67, 84

personality la personalità 16, 17

person la persona 40

performance lo spettacolo 110

perfect perfetto♂/perfetta♀ 92

penis il pisello (literally, pea) 38

pee, to pisciare 79

pastel pastello 76

password la password 47, 48

party la festa 12, 13, 16, 17

partner (boyfriend/ girlfriend) il mio ragazzo♂/la mia ragazza♀ 35, 44, 85, 86

parking il parcheggio 88, 89

pants i pantaloni 68, 70, 71, 72, 73

panties le mutandine 70

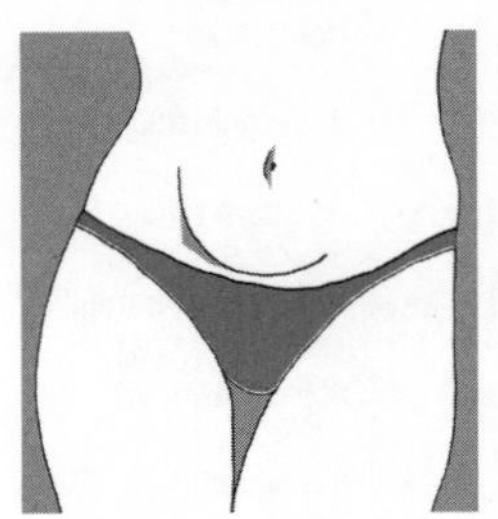

painting il quadro (art on display) 74, 75, 76, 102

package il pacco 38

oven il forno 75

outfit il vestito 70

out fuori 34, 35

ouch ahi 23

other altro♂/altra♀ 29, 88, 89

opera l'opera 110

online	online 47, 49
old-fashioned	antico♂/antica♀ 51
old	vecchio♂/vecchia♀ 15, 24, 26, 100
OK	OK 34, 35, 36, 51, va bene 35, 36, 51, 104
often	spesso 42, 43, 44
offer	l'offerta 101
offended	offeso♂/offesa♀ 9
of course	certo 88

N

number	numero 44, 45
nudist	il/la nudista 86
now	ora 47, 51, 78, 84
novel	il romanzo (book) 112
nothing	niente 34, 108, 109
not	non 10, 20, 21, 22, 23, 31, 35, 37, 41, 42, 44, 45, 49, 51, 52, 55, 63, 66, 68, 69, 71, 73, 74, 77, 78, 85, 88, 93, 95, 98, 100, 101, 104, 106, 106, 113, 120, 121
nose	il naso 79
no one	nessuno 35, 110
no fucking way	stocazzo 💣 113, sticazzi 💣 113, 120, 121
nipples	i capezzoli 38
night	la notte 52, 53, la serata (from evening on) 95
newspaper	il quotidiano 111, il giornale 111, 112
new	nuovo♂/nuova♀ 20, 63, 72, 120, 121
never	mai 20, 23, 37, 112
network	la rete 120, 121
nervous	nervoso♂/nervosa♀ 37
nerd	il/la nerd 50, 118
neighbor	il vicino♂/la vicina♀ 20, 22
neck	il collo 78
near	vicino 31, 32
nature	la natura 31
national park	il parco nazionale 87
name	il nome 112

M

my, mine	mio♂/mia♀ 19, 20, 23, 24, 25, 35, 42, 49, 55, 60, 66, 75, 81, 85, 86, 98, 101, 104
my parents	i miei 26, 84
mute	muto♂/muta♀ 64
musical	musical 110
music video	il videoclip 65
music	la musica 16, 49, 65, 95, 104
museum	il museo 85
mug	la tazza 82, 102
much	molto♂/molta♀ 16, 17
MP3 player	il lettore mp3 61

MP3 l'mp3 60, 61, 62

movie il film 12, 13, 65, 86, 106, 107, 108

mouth la bocca 78

mouse il mouse 60, 61, 66

money i soldi, 97, 99, 100 il denaro (official) 97, la pilla (Genoa) 97, la lira (old Italian currency) 97, 98, 100, la moneta (official) 97, 98, la grana 97, 98

momma, your tua madre 113, 116

mom ma' 24, mamma 23, 25, mami 24

modern moderno♂/moderna♀ 75

mobile il cellulare 51, 53, 54, 60, 61, 63, 64, 66, 67, 88, 89, il telefonino 61, 62, 66

missionary missionaria 39

mirror lo specchio 31, 71, 73, 74, 75, 76

mint la menta 94

minimalist minimalista 75

milk il latte 94

microwave il microonde 37, 75

message il messaggio 49, 53, 54, 63, 64

mess il casino 20, 21, 22, 98, lo shfacimm' (Campania) 119

menu il menù 64, 65

melons i meloni (breasts, fruit) 38, le tette (breasts) 38, 44

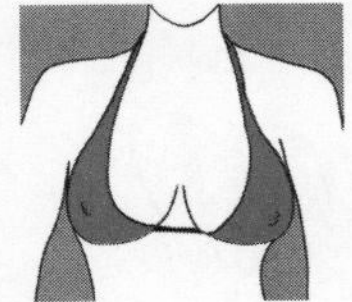

meet, to incontrare 55

me me 20, 29, 35, 81, 101, mi 21, 33, 35, 47, 52, 63, 77, 79, 82, 101, 110, 114,

match partita (sports) 95

masturbate, to toccarsi (touch oneself) 39, farsi una sega 39

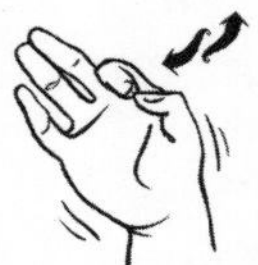

martial arts le arti marziali 106

married sposato♂/sposata♀ 23

many molti♂/molte♀ 31, 32, 88, 89

man l'uomo 31, 32, 102

mall il centro commerciale 72

make love, to fare l'amore 39, farlo 39, 40, 45

magazine la rivista 111, 112

luggage i bagagli 89, 90, 91

luck la fortuna 19

lover l'amante 42, 44, 45, 120, 121

love, to make fare l'amore 39

love, to amare 41, 42, 43, 121, adorare (to adore) 23, 85

love l'amore 20, 39, 41, 42, 50, 53, 77, 78, l'affetto (friends and family) 37

lost perso♂/persa♀ 36, 85, 108, 109

loser lo sfigato♂/la sfigata♀ 11, 12, 13, 15, 17, 19, 43

look like, to sembrare (to appear) 71

loogey lo scaracchio 79

long lungo♂/lunga♀ 110

log out, to terminare la sessione 49

log in, to loggarsi 50

loaded pieno♂/piena♀ 23, 44, 79, 93, 96, 99, 100, bombato♂/bombata♀ 99, ricco♂/ricca♀ 99, 100, avere il portafogli gonfio 100

live, to vivere 23, 55

listen, to ascoltare 104

list la lista 64, 102

liquor l'alcol (in general) 16, 17

link il link 47, 49, 51

lingerie la biancheria intima 102

like, to mi piace/piacciono... (I like...) 31, 32, 49, 66, 68, 74, 95, 104, 111

like better, to preferire (to prefer) 51, 104

lie down, to stendersi 78

lie la bugia 20

lick, to leccare 40

less meno 52

lesbian la lesbica (official) 27, la lella (LGBT lingo) 27, la camionista (slang for manly lesbians) 27

leg la gamba 36, 37

left la sinistra 40

leave vattene (command) 42, 43

last ultimo♂/ultima♀ 88, 101

laptop il portatile 61

language la lingua 65

lamp la lampada 75

ladies' night la serata donne 95

kitten il cucciolo (generic) 19, 20

kitchen la cucina 74, 75, 76

kiss, to baciare 40, baciarsi (each other) 39, sbaciucchiarsi (kiss all over) 39, slinguarsi (French kiss) 39, 45

kiss il bacio 52, 53, 54

keyboard la tastiera 60, 61, 62, 64, 66

keep cool, to (stay calm) stare calmo♂/calma♀ 9, 12

just give a fuck, to fottitinne (Campania) (not to overworry) 119

job il lavoro 53, 54, 72, 77

jewelry shop la gioielleria 102

jewelry i gioielli 100, 102

jerk disgraziato♂/disgraziata♀ 42, mona (Veneto) 119, 122

jeans i jeans 13, 71, 72, 103

jacket la giacchetta (generally women's clothing) 70, 72

jack off, to farsi una sega 39

Italian italiano♂/italiana♀ 37, 53, 55, 59, 101, 104, 110

iPod® l'iPod® 62, 66

invitation l'invito 12

invent, to inventare 60

internet freak il maniaco♂/la maniaca♀ di internet 59

internet l'internet 48, 49, 59, 63, 88, 89

integrated integrato♂/integrata♀ 63, 67

inspiration l'ispirazione 75

inhale, to inspirare 78

indifferent indifferente 37

inconvenient scomodo♂/scomoda♀ 60

inbox la posta in arrivo 54

ignore, to ignorare 66

idiot il/la deficiente 79, 80

ice cube il cubetto di ghiaccio 40

I io 35, 42, 47, 53, 98

hybrid ibrido♂/ibrida♀ 82, 83

husband il marito 24

hurt, to fare male 79

hungry, to be morire di fame (to be starving) 93

hug l'abbraccio 33

how come 20, 29, 30, 34, 35, 47, 50, 56, 57, 63, cosa 20, 29, 47, 60, 71, 72, che (as a question or exclamation) 8, 9, 12, 35, 36, 41, 42, 74, 75, 85

hottie un fico♂/una fica♀ 14, 17

hotel l'hotel 85, 86, 88, 89, 91

hot, to be essere fico♂/fica♀ 9, 13

hot caldo♂/calda♀ (temperature) 81, 82, 92, fico♂/fica♀ (awesome) 8, 9, 10, 13, 36, 37, 38, 51, fosforescente (color) 76

horror l'orrore 106

horoscope l'oroscopo 44

home la casa 12, 13, 74, 75

hold, to trattenere (breath) 78

hit un successo (as in movie blockbuster) 106, 107

high heel (shoe) (la scarpa con) i tacchi alti 70, 72

here qui 35, 55, 63

hello ciao 10, 34, 36, 47, 50, 51, 55, 63, 74, 98, 105, 115, 121, pronto (on the phone) 35, 50, 63

heck, what the porca miseria 117, 118

hear, to sentire 21, 22, 63

health la salute 88

headphones le cuffie 61, 62

head la testa (official) 77, 78, 79

have, to avere 29, 31, 32, 39, 45, 56, 77, 78, 79, 98, 120

have to, to dovere (must) 35, 45, 66, 82, 88, toccare a 98, 99

hate, to odiare 42, 43, 81

hardware store la ferramenta 102

hard-on, to have a avercelo duro 39

happy felice 77, 78

hangover i postumi 79, 80

handsome bello♂/bella♀ 36, 37, 71, 74, bellissimo♂/bellissima♀ (even more handsome) 36

handjob sega 39, pugnetta 119

hand luggage i bagagli a mano 89, 90

hair salon il parrucchiere 103

hair i capelli 35, 45

hacker hacker (technology) 49

guy il tipo 13, 14, 16, 17, 20, 26, 88, il guaglione 14, il tizio (stranger) 14

guest l'ospite 89

guess, to indovinare 20

group il gruppo 53, 54, 95

greetings i saluti 9, 26, 54, 62, 98, 96, 112

green, to be essere ecologista 81

green il verde (color) 44, 76

great benissimo 34, 68

greasy grasso♂/grassa♀ 93

gray il grigio 44, 45

grandpa il nonno 23, 24

grandma la nonna 23, 24, 98, la nonnina (granny) 16, 17

grandfather il nonno 23, 24

graduate, to laurearsi 98

goth il darkettone♂/la darkettona♀ 23

gossip (person) il pettegolo♂/la pettegola♀ 20, il pettegolezzo (info) 20, 21, 22

gorgeous bello♂/bella♀ 36, 37, 71, 74, bellissimo♂/bellissima♀ (even more gorgeous) 36

goody two-shoes il fighetto♂/la fighetta♀ 15, 16, 17, il fichetto♂/la fichetta♀ 15

gold l'oro 100, 102

God Dio 20

go out, to uscire 69

go on a cruise, to essere in crociera 84, 86

go, to andare 25, 43, 64, 77, 93, 104, 115, 117, 118

glasses gli occhiali 23

give, to dare 82, 101

girlfriend la mia/tua/sua ragazza (my/your/his) 35, 44

girl la ragazza 67, la tipa 13, 14, 17

get stuck, to bloccarsi 65, 66

get lost, to levarsi dai piedi 41, 42, 52, 53

genre il genere 104, 106

gay gay 27, 30, 31, 32, finocchio 27, ricchione 27, pazza 31, 32, principessa 31, 33

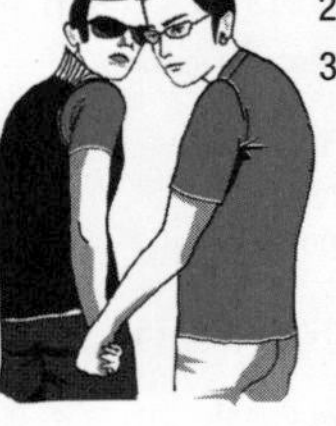

garbage schifo 79, schifezza (statement about something) 11, 106

game il gioco 65

gala il galà 72

gal la tipa 13, 14, 17, la guagliona (southern Italy) 14, la tizia (stranger) 14

gadget l'accessorio 70, 74

F

furniture i mobili 74, 75

funny divertente 106, 107, 110

fun il divertimento 45

full, to be essere pieno 44, 79, 93, 99, 100, stare per esplodere (to be about to explode) 93

fucking cazzo di 💣 11, 92, 114

fuck, what the porca troia 💣 115, 117, 118

fuck up la cazzata 💣 114, 115

fuck off, to andare a fare in culo 115, 117, vaffanculo 💣 115, 117, 118, 120, 122, fanculo 115

fuck, to give a fottersene 💣 119, 120

fuck, to scopare 💣💣 39, 43, 44, fottere 💣💣 82, 113, 119, ficcare 💣💣 39

fuck cazzo 22, 71, 80, 113, 114, 115, 116, 117, 118, 119, 120, 121, 122, figa 💣 (Milan) (exclamation) 115, 116, 117

frozen bloccato♂/bloccata♀ (tech) 66

front davanti 40

from da 47, 48

friend with benefits il trombamico♂/la trombamica♀ 42, 44

friend l'amico♂/l'amica♀ 12, 13, 31, 32, 53, 85, 86, vecchio 15, fra' 15, 25, cumpa' 15, vecio♂/vecia♀ 15

fridge il frigo 75

Friday il venerdì 34, 36, 37, 45, 47

free libero♂/libera♀ 35, gratis (no cost) 88, 89, 95

fossil il fossile 66

forgetful distrattone (friendlier) 23

forever per sempre 52, 53

foot, on a piedi 83

foot il piede 83

fitting room il camerino 70

find, to trovare 31, 47

fiancé fidanzato♂/fidanzata♀ 42

favorite preferito♂/preferita♀ 104

fashion la moda 112

fart, to scorreggiare 80, scoreggiare 79

fan il ventilatore (electric) 75, 76, il ventaglio (hand) 102, il/la fan (music) 121

family la famiglia 16, 17, 23, 74

false falso♂/falsa♀ 21, 63, 75, 105, 110

E

eyeglasses gli occhiali 23

eye l'occhio 78

exhale, to espirare 78

exercise l'esercizio 78

excellent ottimo 120, 121, stupendo 7, 8, 74, 96, 110, eccellente 110

ex ex 20, 45

evening la sera 47, 72, 89

euro (currency) l'euro 95, 97, 101

environment l'ambiente 82

entrance l'ingresso 95

enjoy, to buon appetito (enjoy your meal) 93

English l'inglese 58, 94

end, to terminare 49, 64

enable, to abilitare 49

e-mail la mail 47, 48, 49, 50, 51, 60, 66, la posta elettronica 49, 59, l'email 49

elegant elegante 71

education l'istruzione 53, 54

ecologist l'ecologista 81, 82, 83

eco-friendly eco-compatibile 83

eclectic eclettico♂/eclettica♀ 74, 75

eat, to mangiare 93

D

DVD player il lettore DVD 60

dumbass stronzo 💣💣 14, 113, 116, 122, coglione 💣💣 116, 122

dudette ciccia 18, bella 18, 19

dude ciccio 18, bello 18, 19, capo 18, mister 18

dry secco♂/secca♀ 99

drunk, to get ubriacarsi 86

drunk sballone (drunkard) 15, 16, 17

drink, to bere 79, 80

drink qualcosa da bere 36, 86, 96

dressing room il camerino 70

dress l'abito 70, 72

drama drammatico (film genre) 106

drag queen drag queen 31

download, to scaricare 49, 50, 59, 66

door la porta 75

done ecco fatto (exclamation) 68

dollar il dollaro 91

doggy style alla pecorina 39

document il documento 50

do, to fare 31, 34, 35, 36, 37, 44, 51, 60, 74, 78

do it, to farlo 39, 40, 45

dish il piatto 98, 99

disgusting schifo 12, 81, 93, che schifo 93

discount lo sconto 101

disc il disco 103

directions le indicazioni 85

dinner la cena 17, 34, 47

digital camera la fotocamera digitale 61

diet la dieta 93

die, to morire 55, 77, 81

diarrhea, to have avere la sciolta (slang) 79

diarrhea la sciolta (slang) 79

designer il/la designer 74

design, to arredare (interior) 74, 75

delicious buonissimo♂/buonissima♀ 93

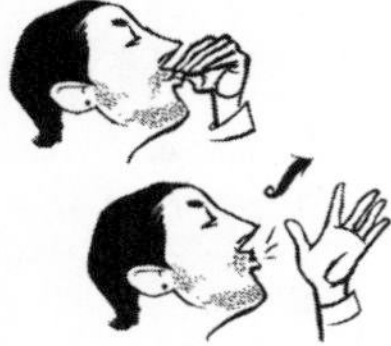

delete, to cancellare 48

deeply profondamente 78

dear caro♂/cara♀ 9, 19, 26, 33, 37, 54, 62, 90, 96, 105, 112, 115

day il giorno 83, 85, 112

daughter la figlia 15, 113

date l'appuntamento 13, 34, 36, 37, 44, 47, 55

darling tesoro 19, 20, 41

dark scuro (color) 76

dance, to ballare 72, 96

dance club la discoteca 95, 96, 97

dance il ballo 16, 17

damn cazzo di 63, 88

daddy il papi 24

dad il papà 15, 23

curtains le tendine 75, 76

curse la parolaccia (vulgar word) 113, 115, 116

cunt la passera 38

cruise la crociera 84, 86

crotch il pacco (literally, package) (male) 38, la fica (female) 9, 31, 38

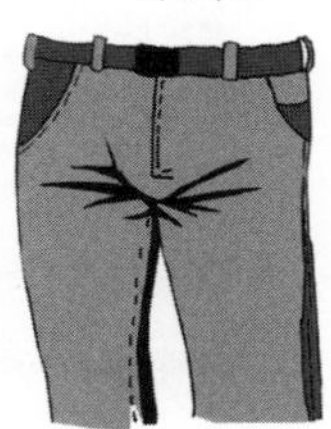

critic il critico♂/la critica♀ 107

cream la panna (food) 94

crazy pazzo♂/pazza♀ 31, 32

crappy cazzo di 11, schifo di 71

crabs le piattole (disease) 79, 80

coward quaquaraqua (slang) 115

cover la copertura 31, 32, 33, la fica-specchio (Tuscany) (gay life) 31

cousin il cugino♂/la cugina♀ 23

couple la coppia 31, 32, 44

countryside la campagna 85, 86

corner l'angolo 12, 13

cordially cordialmente 19

cool fico 8, 9, 10, 13, 14, figata 7, 9, 10, 12, 13, 106, spacca 7, 10, 13, 23, meraviglioso 8, fantastico 8, stupendo 7, 8, troppo bello 8, bella lì 8, fregno (Abruzzo) 8, 'na bumm' (Calabria) 8, che sborata (Emilia-Romagna) 8, 10, che tajo (Rome) 8, 9, da paura 8, 9, 10, figo 8, 10, 88, 89, 96, 104, comanda (Sicily) 8, spacchiuso (Sicily) 8, ganzo (Tuscany) 8, che spettacolo (exclamation or state of being) 8; un figo♂/ una figa♀ 106; fresco (temperature) 7

contacts contatti 65, rubrica (phone book) 64

connected connesso♂/connessa♀ 47, 48, 67

confused confuso♂/confusa♀ 9

condom il gommino (rubber) 79

concert il concerto 95, 104, 110

computer il computer 61, 62, 66, il pc 61, 62, il portatile (laptop) 61

composer il compositore/la compositrice 65

complementary incluso (service) 88

comic strip vignette (short strips) 111, 112, fumetti (books) 111

comfortable comodo♂/comoda♀ 74, 77, 78

comedy la commedia 106, 107, 108, 112

come out of the closet, to fare outing 29, 30, fare coming out 29

come, to venire (with or without sexual implications) 39, 104

combination accostamento (colors) 75

color il colore 44, 45, 74, 75

cold freddo♂/fredda♀ 85, 92

coin la moneta (in slang, also meaning money in general) 97, 98

coffee table il tavolino 75

coffee il caffè 82

cocktail il cocktail 95

cocksucker il/la succhiacazzi 117

cock il cazzo 39

coat il cappotto 70, la giacca 70

club il club (private) 97, la discoteca (dance) 95, 96, 97

clothing i vestiti 81

closet l'armadio 75

close, to chiudere 95

clock l'orologio 65

click, to cliccare 48, 51, fare click 47, 48

cleavage la scollatura 68, 70

classic il classico 75, 111, 112

circus il circo 110

chick una fica (hot girl) 14

cheers salute 80

check, to controllare 47, 48, 66

chat, to chattare 47, 48, 51, 52, 53

change, to cambiare 63, 69, 120, 121

change gli spiccioli (money) 97

chandelier il candeliere 75

chair la sedia 75

chain (mail) la catena 51

cell phone il cellulare 51, 53, 54, 60, 61, 63, 64, 66, 67, 88, 89, il telefonino 61, 62, 66

ceiling il soffitto 74

catch, to beccare (meet) 47, 49

cash contanti 99, gli spiccioli (loose change) 97

case il caso (situation) 120, 121

carry-on luggage i bagagli a mano 89, 90

care, to importare 101, prendersi cura di (take care of)

car l'auto 83, la macchina 22

can (verb) potere 20, 31, 35, 49, 51, 55, 88, 102, 104, 106, 116

camping, to go andare in campeggio 72

camping il campeggio 72

calm calmo♂/calma♀ 9, 12

call, to chiamare 34, 35, 37, 51, 64

call la chiamata 64, 66

calendar il calendario 65

cabbage il cavolo 117, 118

buy, to comprare 49, 102

butt il culo 9, 33, 38, 44, 68, 71, 73, 117

but ma 10, 44, 47, 60, 69, 73, 98, 120, 121, però 51, 68, 104, 107

business gli affari (often used in plural form) 90

buns le chiappe, il culo 💣 (butt cheeks) 38

bungler l'imbranato ♂/l'imbranata ♀ 50

bum il/la pezzente 71, 98, 99, 100

bullshit la stronzata 💣 119, 122

brown-noser il/la leccaculo 💣 115, 122

brother il fratello 19, 20, il fratellino (little brother) 23

broke, to be essere al verde 98, 99, 100, non avere una lira (to be bankrupt) 98, 100

bright brillante (color) 76

break, to rompere 113

bra il reggiseno 69, 70

boyfriend il mio/tuo/suo ragazzo (my/your/her) 35, 44, 85, 86

boy il ragazzo 67, il tipo (slang) 13, 14, 17

boxer shorts i boxer 70

boutique hotel il boutique hotel 85, 86

bottom passivo (passive, sexual position) 31, sedere (ass) 38

boring noioso♂/noiosa♀ 110

boot lo stivale 70

bookworm il topo di biblioteca 111, 112

bookstore la libreria 102

bookshelf la libreria 75

book il libro 53, 65, 111, 112

bone l'osso 36

body il corpo 36, il fisico 68

Blu-ray player il lettore Blu-ray 61

blue il blu 45, 76

blouse la camicetta 68, 70, 71, 72

bloggers i blogger 49, 55, 56

blog, to bloggare 55, 56

blockbuster il successone 106

block il blocco (stop) 65

blind date l'appuntamento al buio 55

black il nero 45, 76

bitch la troia 115, la puttana 113, 114, 115, 117, 118, 119, 122

bisexual il/la bisessuale (official) 27, il/la bisex 27, 28

bikini il bikini 68

bike la bicicletta 88, 89, la bici (abbreviation) 83

best il/la migliore 23, 96, il meglio 55, 56, 76

belt la cintura 69, 70

believe, to credere 20

beer la birra 95

beep il bip (sound) 63, 120, 121

bedroom la camera da letto 74, 75, 76

bed, to go to andare a letto 39, 43, 45

bed il letto 39, 43, 44, 45, 74, 75, 76

because perché 63

beautiful bello♂/bella♀ 37, 71, 74, bellissimo♂/bellissima♀ (even more beautiful) 36, 85

bear l'orso (animal) 31, 32

beach la spiaggia 12, 13, 74, 85, 86, 87

be, to essere 7, 8, 9, 10, 11, 20, 23, 29, 30, 31, 32, 34, 35, 36, 37, 42, 43, 44, 45, 47, 48, 49, 50, 51, 52, 53, 55, 56, 57, 60, 63, 66, 71, 73, 74, 75, 77, 78, 79, 80, 81, 82, 83, 85, 86, 88, 89, 92, 93, 95, 96, 98, 99, 100, 101, 104, 106, 107, 108, 109, 110, 114, 116, 117, 118, 120, 121

battery la batteria 66

bathing suite il costume da bagno 70

bastard il bastardo 113, 122

bar il bar 88, 89

band il gruppo (as in rock) 95

balls le palle (male anatomy) 38, 113, 114, i coglioni 39, 113, 117, 118, i maroni (nuts) 118, cojoni (Rome) 119

ballet il balletto 110

ballerina la ballerina 110z

bag la borsa 81, 82, 89, 90

bad words le parolacce 113, 115, 116

backpacking, to go andare zaino in spalla 85, 86

backpack lo zaino 89, 90

back door da dietro 39

back dietro (position) 39, schiena (body part) 79, indietro (movement) 64, 65

baby bimbo♂/bimba♀ 19, 20, piccolo♂/piccola♀ 19

A

awful brutto♂/brutta♀ 11, 12, uno schifo 110

awesome fighissimo♂/fighissima♀ 85

author l'autore♂/l'autrice♀ 65

aunt la zia 23

atmosphere l'ambiente 82, l'atmosfera 95

asshole lo stronzo♂/la stronza♀ 14, 113, 114, 116, 122, cugghione (Puglia) 119

ass il culo 9, 33, 38, 44, 68, 71, 73, 117

ask, to chiedere 85, domandare 120, 121

ASAP il prima possibile 66

artist l'artista 65, 102, 103

art l'arte 75

arrogant antipatico (unpleasant) 23, presuntuoso 115, sborone (show-off, Emilia-Romagna) 115, 122

army knife il coltellino svizzero 68

area la zona 66

appliances gli elettrodomestici 75

apartment l'appartamento 20, 75

anything qualsiasi cosa 12

angel l'angelo 19, 20

amenities i servizi 88

ambiguous ambiguo♂/ambigua♀ 31, 32, 33

also anche 10, 69, 88, 89, 104

alone da solo♂/da sola♀ 23

all tutto 83, 85

album l'album 65

air, central l'aria condizionata 83

air l'aria 83

affair la storia d'amore 106, la tresca (secret) 29, 30

adventure l'avventura (also meaning a one-night stand) 85

address l'indirizzo 48

addicted, to be rimanerci sotto 108

action l'azione 106, 108

achy pieno♂/piena♀ di acciacchi 23

account l'account 56, 57

according to secondo 74, 111

accessory l'accessorio 70, 74

a lot molto♂/molta♀ 16, 88